Seeing Beyond

BIPOLAR STIGMA

The person, not the prejudice.

DAVID A. FEINGOLD, ED.D

ISBN 979-8-218-56637-1 (pbk.)

BISAC Subjects (in order of relevance):
PSY022030 PSYCHOLOGY / Psychopathology /
Bipolar Disorder
BIO026000 BIOGRAPHY & AUTOBIOGRAPHY /
Memoirs
PSY068000 PSYCHOLOGY / Psychotherapy / Art
& Music Therapy

Front cover,
Book Design & Illustrations
by David A. Feingold

Published in the United States
by David A. Feingold

"Inspiring and Illuminating."
- Reader's Favorite 5 STARS

"I recommend this book to the relatives and friends of bipolar patients; they need to understand what it feels like for their relative or friend with bipolar disorder and how to help them live an integrated life."
- Online Book Club 5 STARS

"An absolutely essential read for anyone with an interest in bipolar and how it affects either themselves or those around them."
- Reader's Favorite 5 STARS

"When I ask,
where is my soul,
how do I meet it,
what does it want now?
The answer is,
turn to your images."

–James Hillman
Father of Archetypal Psychology

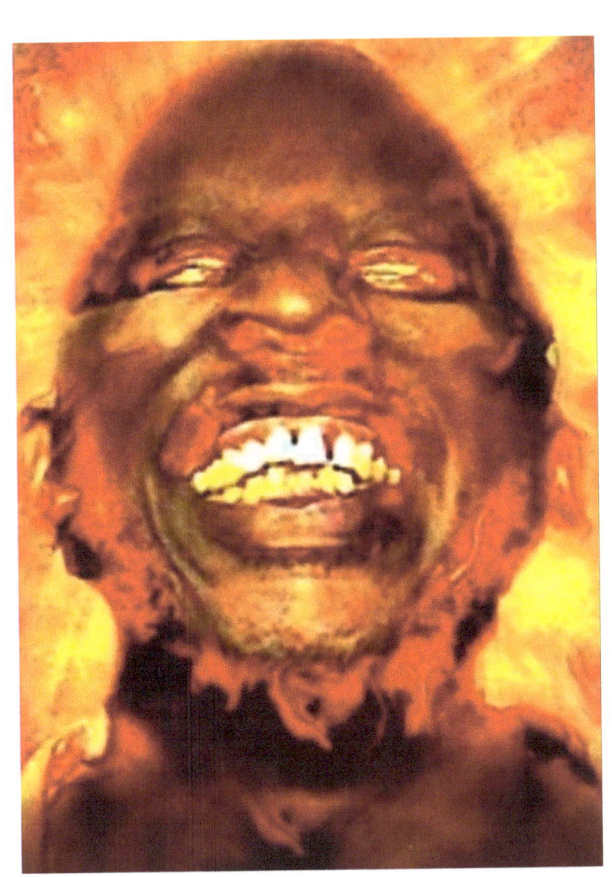

Contents

Dedication

For Amie Cohen

By Elana Cohen

My mother committed suicide in 2005 after decades of living with and suffering from bipolar disorder, leaving behind her two daughters, my older sister, 18, and myself, 15 at the time, a grieving husband, aging parents, and a shocked and saddened community. Throughout the years, I have tried to come up with ways to mourn my mother and help others at the same time.

People have been trying to break the stigma of mental illness for a long time. If you have not experienced some sort of mental illness, it can be hard to understand what it feels like to be mentally ill. I could not wrap my head around the fact that depression, or what I thought was just depression, drove her to leave us.

When you have a parent who died because of mental illness, the scariest thing to think about is, "What if this happens to me?" I spent years being mad at my mother, not understanding why she did what she did. It took me nine years to finally realize how much she was hurting and how she could not find her way out of the darkness caused by her bipolar disorder.

I feel that I need to speak up and fight. Fight to end the negative stigma of mental illness. Mental illness does not define who you are. It is a part of you, but not everything. I truly hope this book and resources like it can help make a difference and urge people to get help when they need it. No one should ever have to suffer in silence, and everyone should have a fighting chance at life.

Mom, "I will love you forever. I'll like you for always. As long as I'm living, my mommy you'll be." ("Love You Forever" by Robert Munsch)

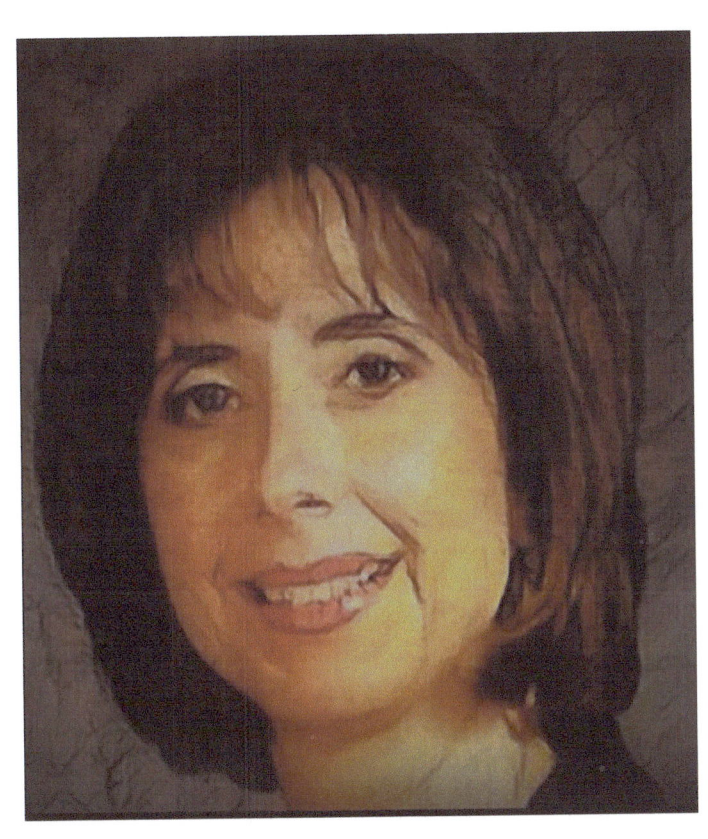

Preface

Ending Stigma

Early in my doctoral research in Disability Studies, I felt compelled to create something meaningful—something that could support people living with mental illness and those who care about them. I also hoped to contribute to the fields of education, psychology, social work, medicine, and beyond—disciplines deeply invested in promoting mental well-being. I believe that goal has been realized in this book.

This work offers a window into how art can help heal the emotional wounds of mental illness. It also introduces a key concept I call the Impaired Self—a self shaped by stigma and the challenges of navigating life with a psychiatric diagnosis.

Through personal vignettes, I illustrate how stigma erodes dignity, and how self-worth can be reclaimed. These stories bring immediacy to the lived experience of mental illness and highlight what is often invisible to the public eye.

I ask you, the reader, to suspend any assumptions or stereotypes you may hold about mental disorders. Enter, just for a while, our often-hidden world. And from there, allow yourself to be informed—and perhaps transformed—by a deeper understanding of the barriers we face, not only from within but from a society that too often misunderstands us.

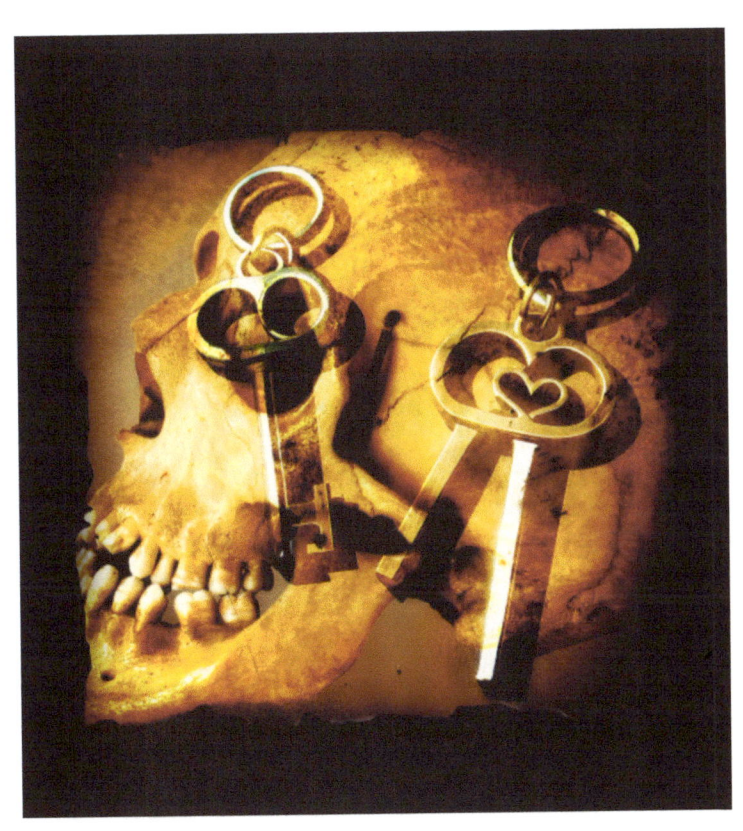

Acknowledgment

With Gratitude

To the **Institute of Design at the Illinois Institute of Technology**, where I first learned about design in the Bauhaus tradition.

To **Loyola University School of Social Work**, where I gained deep insight into mental illness and its functioning within the social environment.

To my late sister, **Bonnie**, who dragged me to an art class over fifty years ago—my first hint that I might have artistic ability.

To my mother, **Frances**, for her lifelong intellectual encouragement. At 94, in the final year of her life, she said, "I never knew you were this intelligent!"

To **Dr. Robert Greendale**, my psychiatrist for over a decade, who supported me through thick and thin and told me I would one day contribute meaningfully to the mental health field.

To **Dr. Terry Smith**, Director of the Doctoral Program in Disability Studies at National Louis University and my dissertation chair, who recognized the value of my art and validated the concept of the Bipolar Impaired Self.

To **Joyce and Dusty Licht Sang**, founders of the Ryan Licht Sang Bipolar Foundation, for their tireless work to end bipolar stigma—and for including my work in their annual Insights exhibit.

To **Professor Paul Grobstein** of Bryn Mawr College, who enthusiastically featured my work on his groundbreaking neurobiology website, Serendip, years before his passing.

To **Beth Levin**, for your creative insights, steady encouragement, and unwavering belief in the purpose of this book.

To **Tom, Rachel, and Elana Cohen**, for showing the resilience of the human spirit in the face of bipolar challenges.

And to my children, **Hadar** and **Seth**, who inspire me every day to be and do my best. Your inspiration continues…

First Things First

Person or Disability First

An artist with bipolar disorder or bipolar artist?

Person-first language is a widely accepted convention—seen as more respectful and dignified than identifying someone by their diagnosis. But in this case, I don't follow it. My use of "bipolar" as an identity-first term is both personal and purposeful.

The rejection of illness-first language is a social construct shaped by mental health professionals, academics, disability advocates, and DEI leaders. It was one of the first principles emphasized in my Disability Studies doctoral program.

Disabled Veteran — Cancer Patient — Bipolar Artist

Which phrase doesn't belong? According to convention, "Bipolar Artist" is incorrect—it should be "a person with bipolar disorder," just as we now say "a person with autism."

But "Disabled Veterans" and "Cancer Patients" are granted empathy and respect, and by extension, their conditions are too. Society allows those identities to come first. People with bipolar disorder rarely receive the same regard.

Social convention shouldn't override individual choice—especially when language, like identity, evolves.

"Queer." "Crip." "Mad." People are taking back once-held derogatory language and legitimizing it so that we, behind the descriptors, can finally be declared "legitimate."

Epigraph

Sinclair Ceaser III

"Now for the part that turned my entire life upside down. My psychiatrist said, "Based on everything we now know, I'm diagnosing you with Bipolar I." After we talked about medication, side effects, follow-up appointments, and what this all meant for my life moving forward, I jetted to the parking lot to call my wife.

Paranoia set in somewhere between flying out of the lobby and unlocking the door to my Corolla.

It was hard to breathe, not only because of how cold it was outside, but also because of the panic. My wife, supportive and patient on her end of the call, had been through the worst of my episode. I was thankful I had her in my corner because the news was too much to digest. I recounted the appointment and begged her not to tell anyone about my bipolar disorder diagnosis. Shame was at the root of my plea. Invisible walls were closing in."

Introduction

An End Requires A Beginning

The beginning of this book also marks the beginning of the end.

The end of silently accepting outdated, harmful beliefs, behaviors, and speech toward people with mental illness. The end of stigma—through understanding the Bipolar Impaired Self.

To the clinical and non-clinical professionals who support those with mental illness every day: I hope this book serves as a meaningful companion in your vital work. Introducing the concept of the Impaired Self at the university level—across medicine, psychiatry, psychology, social work, counseling, and education—would be especially valuable.

If we're to create lasting change in how society views mental illness, we must all contribute:

We can raise awareness of the Impaired Self and the stigma that shapes it.

We can examine how schools and systems reinforce that stigma—and learn how to reverse it.

We can look people in the eye.

We can listen.

We can offer support.

We can be a light in the dark—and a shield of love to help protect someone from themselves.

We can stand up.

We can stay committed.

We can help build a stronger, healthier sense of self for those with mental illness—like never before imagined.

Consider this book your first step.

The Bipolar Impaired Self

Braving The Storms

The Bipolar Impaired Self is the gale force winds of mental illness. It brings dizzying instability and extreme imbalance—leaving you directionless and powerless, like a ship adrift, at the mercy of nature's fury.

I had to right myself—regain control, reclaim my lost identity, and chart a new course. I did so by making pictures. I poured out my feelings and captured them as visual images. That creative act gave me buoyancy, keeping me afloat through every future storm.

There is a story behind my Impaired Self. A sequence of events marked by the chaos of the bipolar experience. It's a story told through my artwork, mapped along a timeline that begins with a sinking ship and continues as a lifelong journey, navigating the uncharted waters of mental illness.

Shadowy Story

A Bipolar Adventure Begins

I once had a shadowy story within me—a vague narrative lying dormant beneath the trap door of my consciousness.

Understanding this hidden cache of personal madness became the quest of my art-based doctoral research in Disability Studies. It is also the foundation of this book.

My task was to probe the depths of my personal, impassioned, dark, and moody artwork to better understand my sense of self—and the emotions, thoughts, and feelings associated with my diagnosis of bipolar disorder. I knew I was on the right path.

As philosophy researcher Max Van Manen explains: "Although a person is potentially able to talk about bodily experiences and subsequently conjure up a 'representation'... every word kills and becomes the death of the object it tries to represent."

If that is the case—if words alone cannot accurately express my bipolar experience how could I find a means of expression with any hope of success?

By making pictures.

Foreword

Joyce and Dusty Sang
Co-Founders
The Ryan Licht Sang Bipolar Foundation

We met David Feingold through his remarkable artwork—bold, deeply felt, and unafraid to confront the rawness of living with bipolar disorder. His images struck a powerful chord with us, reminiscent of the many voices that too often go unheard.

Over the years, we've watched David's journey unfold—not just as an artist, but as someone who channels his experience into something meaningful for others.

Seeing Beyond Bipolar Stigma is the culmination of that journey, and a powerful act of truth-telling. It brings together personal narrative, visual expression, and deep insight into what it means to live with bipolar disorder in a world that still misunderstands it.

This book is not only a testimony to David's lived experience—it is a beacon for others. For families, clinicians, educators, and individuals living with the disorder, this book offers both challenge and hope. It insists that we look beyond labels and see the whole human being.

We are honored to write this Foreword, and prouder still to stand alongside David in the effort to break stigma, promote early understanding, and celebrate the often-hidden strengths of those living with bipolar disorder.

In Ryan's memory, and with hope for the future,
Joyce and Dusty Sang
The Ryan Licht Sang Bipolar Foundation

CHAPTER 1

Welcome To
Being Bipolar

Self-Discovery
Making Pictures
Inner Experience

My Loyal Vanguard

I created "My Loyal Vanguard" when I coined the term "Bipolar Impaired Self." This image reflects the emotional toll of a stigma-infused identity—beaten down, tattered, and shadowed by a sense of defeat. The figure's strong outward presence stands in stark contrast to his sorrowful appearance, revealing the inner rupture of the Impaired Self.

"I'm bipolar, but I'm not crazy, and I never was. I'm stark raving sane."
                                                        –Emilie Autumn

While working on my dissertation, something struck me about my dark, brooding bipolar artwork—something Aristotle once hinted at. He said, "The aim of art is to represent not the outward appearance of things, but their inward significance." So what, then, is the inner significance of my art?

It's this: beyond the clinical symptoms and personal turmoil of psychiatric impairments lies a deeper wound—the emotional pain of what I call the Impaired Self.

The Bipolar Impaired Self is embodied in the artwork shown here, titled My Loyal Vanguard. Like a king's steadfast bodyguard, the Vanguard absorbs the blows—emotional, social, and spiritual—that come from stigma and misunderstanding. On the battlefield of life, while the "king" fights to survive, the Vanguard endures the bruises and emotional battering in silence.

But eventually, even the most loyal defender breaks down. Tattered and torn, the Vanguard—our inner defender—suffers deeply. This, too, is the Impaired Self: the part of us that quietly bears the emotional scars others don't see.

Technology of the Self

Just because we can't see emotional wounds doesn't mean they're not there. Think of the world's most powerful telescopes and microscopes. They reveal distant galaxies and hidden cellular structures—realities invisible without the right lens.

In a similar way, I see my dark art as a kind of technology of the self. Through these visceral, often unsettling images, I invite you to peer into the deepest recesses of the embattled Impaired Self. They are like psychological nebulae or cellular traumas—unseen until magnified through art.

These emotional burdens exist in addition to the known symptoms of bipolar disorder—mania, depression, mood instability. This book does not aim to explain the diagnostic criteria or clinical features of bipolar disorder. That information is widely available through books, podcasts, and videos, many of which I've listed in the Resources and References section.

Instead, I focus here on the lived, internal experience—the part that hides behind diagnoses and stigma. The part that bleeds quietly.

Depressed Person–Look Out Below

There's as much emotional life in a depressed state as there is physical life in a body after a sixty-story fall onto pavement. You are empty, void, and nowhere to be found—by yourself or anyone else.

There's only the vacuum of a life you used to have, a name you used to claim, a person you used to know—now stripped of everything you used to be. As if all the planets, stars, and light itself had been sucked into a black hole in an abandoned universe.

This condition is often called an illness or disorder. But that's like calling World War II a spat or the Inquisition bullying. Bipolar depression is a monster. All the horror stories you knew as a child rolled into one blazing entity that burns through your consciousness and takes up residence inside you.

It takes over—in the form of emptiness. And when it leaves, all that remains is the smoldering.

Schooled

Being depressed at home is one thing. Being depressed at work is quite another. As an elementary school social worker, there were days I'd drive halfway to work—then turn around and head back home because I couldn't face the faces, especially the children. Most of them smiled, giggled, and expected good humor in return. I either had to dodge them by taking a different stairwell or force a smile out of thin air. It worked—unless the principal came looking for me.

It's the "Principle"

That's just what happened to me. It was a Magnet school where the staff were expected to work twice as hard as others in the district, regardless of task or activity. Our school had an outstanding reputation for superior teaching and learning in a community, with most schools failing national academic standards.

One day, I was at school and feeling particularly comatose. Despite my warped brain chemistry daring me to make it to the end of the school day, I had a ton of paperwork to do. It happened to be Halloween when all the children wore costumes for their annual parade down the halls. Teachers, specials, and parents applauded and waved as each "whatever-they-were" passed by.

I suddenly heard the echo of footsteps coming down the hall as a feeling of dread overtook me. In addition to having to deal with my already vulnerable emotional state, my intuition told me things were about to get worse. And they did.

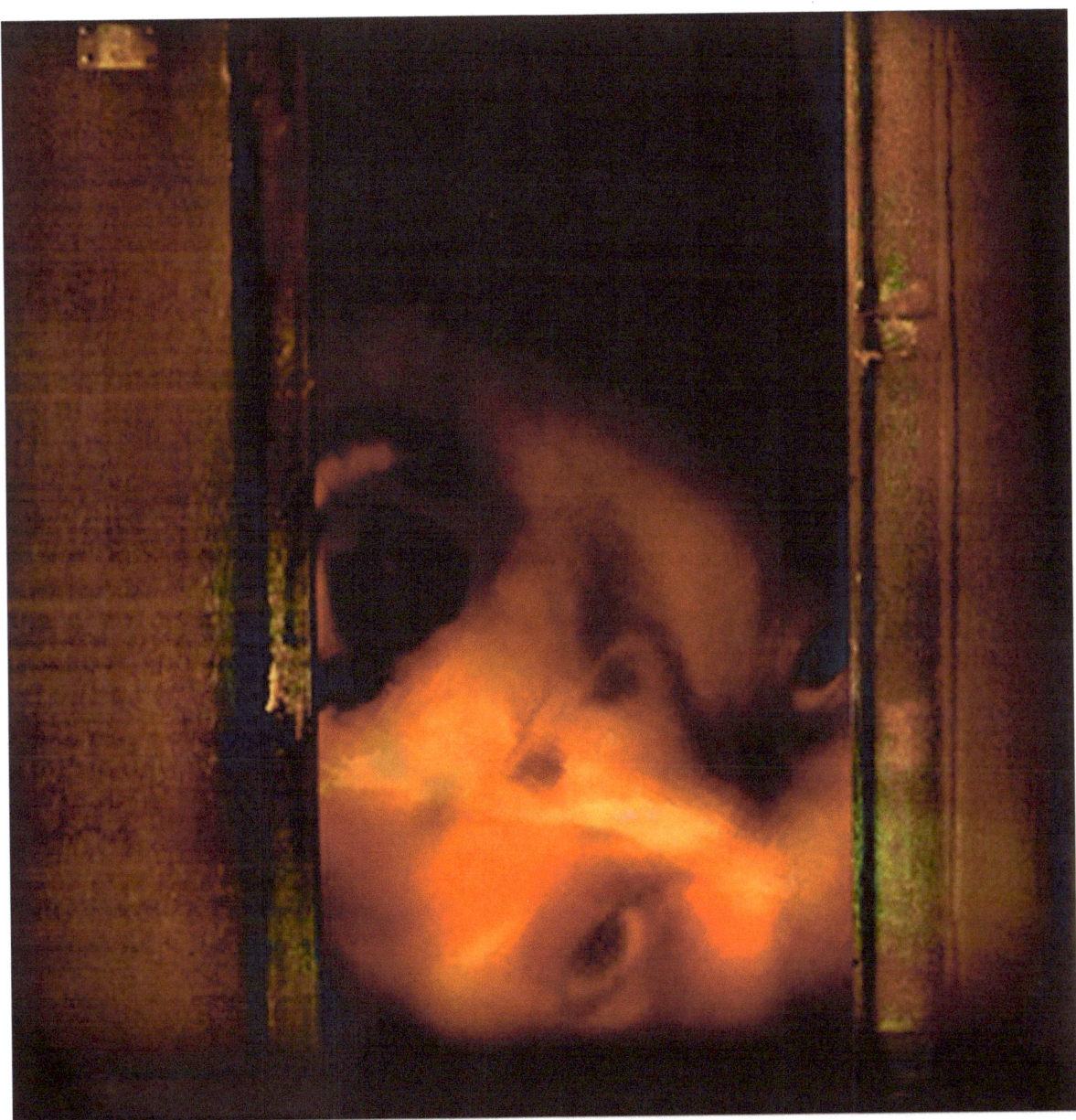

Hitting Rock Bottom
There is no mistaking the feeling of hitting rock bottom in a major bipolar depression.
A depressive state that is so intense, dark, and deep that it is both physically and emotionally painful. You crash, thinking you will never come out of it. When you do, there is a sigh of relief, but it feels short-lived because the next depressive episode could be just around the corner.

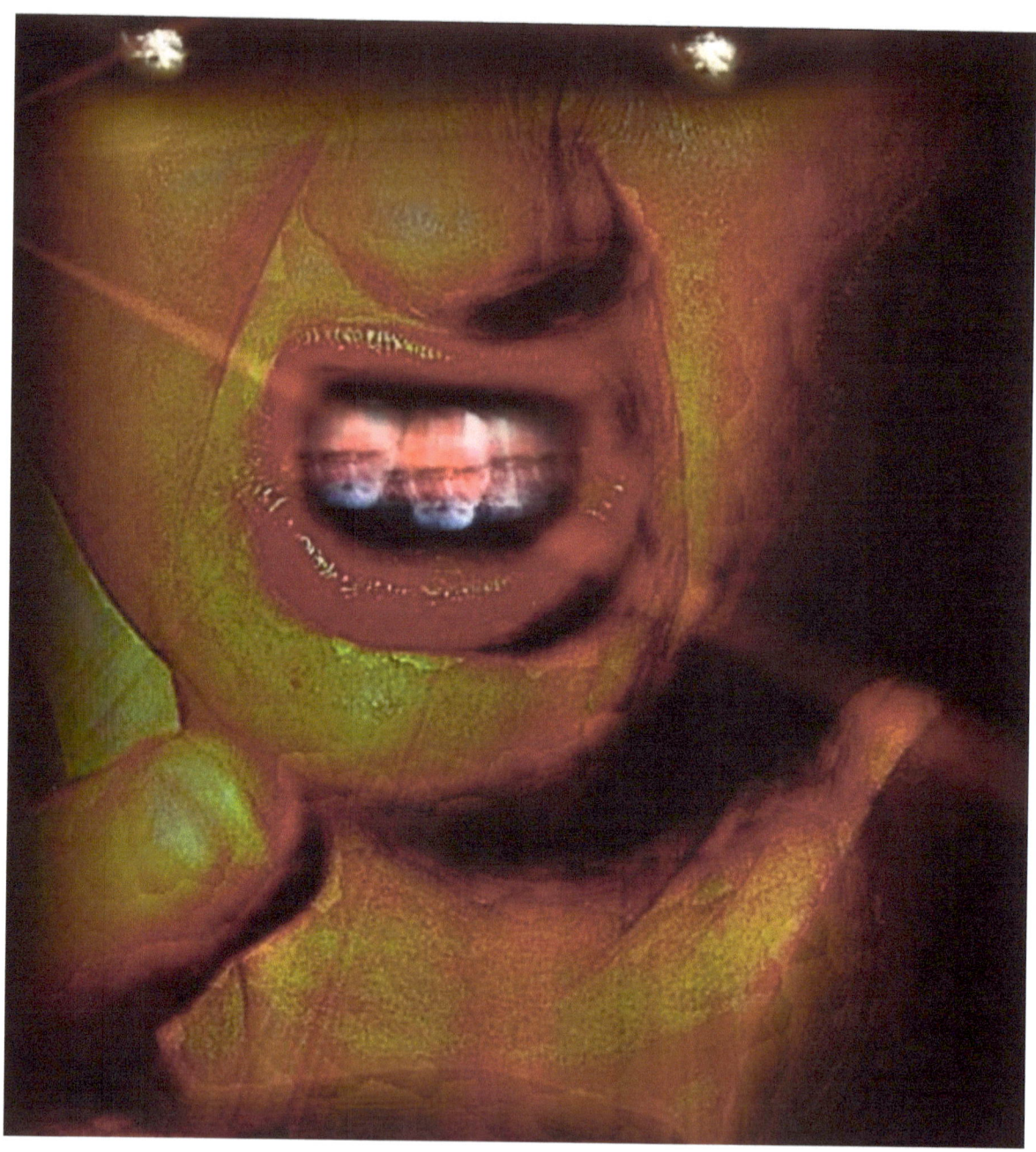

Chewed Out
My principal was irate when I wasn't present to cheer the students on during their hallway Halloween parade. I didn't appreciate her giving me lip, especially since I was behind it.

Here Comes Trouble

It was my principal reading me the riot act for being holed up in my office instead of being a team player and cheering the children on. She was beyond angry to the point of being hostile, shouting, "Our previous social worker participated!!!" Emotional numbing from my depression insulated me from her bitter acrimony.

Mania

Ah, mania, sweet mania! It's a "natural" high that can't be measured by ordinary means because it is the opposite of its evil twin, depression. How do you describe the opposite of total personal emptiness?

How do you explain feeling happiness, confidence, creativity, and energy, as if you had chugged a gallon of Red Bull, twenty Starbuck Grándes and downed two dozen Krispy Kremes all in one sitting?

Manic Moments

Just like its opposite, depression, mania can last anywhere between days, weeks, or even months. Days without sleep. Days filled with doing things you would never have done if you didn't have the diagnosis of bipolar disorder.

Typical behaviors and vices associated with manic phases are pressured speech, feelings of grandeur, exaggerated and unrealistic sense of one's abilities, drug and alcohol binges, spending sprees, social inappropriateness, verbal aggressiveness, sudden obsessive interest and immersion in religion, sleeplessness, extreme impulsivity, irritability, hypersexuality, and denial of one's own malfunctioning.

It's a storm dressed up as brilliance.

So What's it Like?

I have answered three hundred questions with well over a million views regarding bipolar disorder on Quora, a social media question and answer website. My most visited response pertains to whether or not bipolar disorder is real.
This is my answer:

> "I can understand why someone might ask that question, who doesn't have bipolar disorder and doesn't understand the explanations given in texts. Bipolar disorder is very real and then again, it isn't. What I mean by that is best provided by an example of what I've experienced. The part that is real, is the grip that the illness has on people. It really does cause severe debilitating depressions, where you can feel cut off from people and life itself.

The manic aspect of bipolar disorder is also very real. It causes pain and misery in its wake. You can read about this many places online that talk about bipolar disorder. The way it isn't real is how you feel about yourself and the illness after coming out of a depressive or manic episode. Specifically, I am talking about the feeling that what just occurred wasn't the real you. It is as if you've become another person that holds no resemblance to yourself. It also feels unreal, when you question how can something so destructive be so much a part of your life? Sometimes you just sit there in disbelief and its reality is difficult to accept."

BIPOLAR DISORDER: THE LONG AND SHORT

Bipolar disorder is a biological disease in which there are abnormal shifts of elevated and depressed moods caused by alterations in brain chemistry. These occur in periods of mood episodes. Some with bipolar disorder can go years without symptoms, while others can have continual or frequent mild mood swings lasting from days to weeks.

Bipolar 1

Severe and presents as mania and depression.

Bipolar 2

Less intense than Bipolar I, with milder bouts of mania that alternate with more severe depression.

Cyclothymia

Presents as more moderate periods of mania and depression and is not as long-lasting.

Rapid Cycling

Characterized by low to high levels of intense mood swings with rapid cycling, lasting anywhere from days to months to years.

Bottom Line

The good news is that bipolar disorder is treatable. With the right combination of medication and talk therapy, many people find stability, rediscover joy, and build meaningful lives.

If you think you might be experiencing symptoms, don't wait—getting an accurate diagnosis early can make all the difference. Left unaddressed, bipolar disorder can become more complicated over time, affecting relationships, work, and overall well-being. But with support and treatment, healing is possible—and so is hope.

Mardi Gras
As if painted up for a grand celebratory day of fun and frolic, a bipolar mask adorns your personality. A once dark, brooding, and foreboding pessimism becomes an outgoing, lavish, colorful, joyous optimism when mania comes to town. But unlike Mardi Gras, it comes more than once a year without warning and returns to the bottomless pit as suddenly as it came.

Poem

Welcome to being bipolar

Mania hit me like lightning

Like a live lobster in a pot

I didn't know I was boiling

I liked feeling like a live wire

With mania, anything goes

Including your sense of reason

But then the polar opposite

Depression sets in, and it is hell

Feels like a dark place forever

An emptiness that can't be filled

One hundred lashes to the heart

And massive lesions to the brain

Welcome to being bipolar

Questions

How do you communicate emotions, thoughts, and feelings? Verbally? Poetically? Visually? Everyday behavior and actions? Are your communications sufficient? Why or why not? How can you improve them?

What is your sense of self? How do your emotions, thoughts, and feelings determine who you are? Do fluctuations of emotions, thoughts, and feelings change your sense of self? If so, what does that feel like?

The Impaired Self is the inner pain and internal emotional counterpart underlying psychiatric and medical diagnoses. Do you have an inner emotional pain you are dealing with regarding an Impaired Self? Do you share this information with others? Why or why not? How might sharing help you? How might it be counter-productive?

CHAPTER 2

I Was Left With Such Raw Feelings

Where It started
How It Happened
Coming Out

Krazy Klassroom
My life is a room in which I dwell. It's been beaten down, battered, and tattered. I do leave the premises and enjoy the outside world, but I only stay out so long. Then I return home where it's familiar and comfortable, albeit sometimes… unbearable.

"I have more concerns about potential risks and vulnerabilities than most people."

–Jessie Buckley

I f the picture to the left were a person, it would be a mother giving birth to her child, for this picture is the birth of my collection of images depicting my inner experience of bipolar disorder. It is the first bipolar image I've ever made, whose progeny now numbers over 400 pictures.

The experience of bipolar disorder is never-ending, so neither are my depictions of it. Like bloodletting, making pictures helps me heal and maintain my sense of control over my diagnosis. This chapter gives an account of the origin of my images. Without the events that led to this first image, there would be no story, no narrative, no art, and no discovery of the Bipolar Stigma-Impaired Self.

The Air Was Thick

It all began in one of my doctoral classes. There was a rather intense discussion among the ten or so students sitting around a cluster of small tables, joined together to form a rectangle for communal exchange. Our professor was at the head of the table.

The discussion, involving a few of the students, had become personal. The subject was race relations, and the professor attempted to steer the class back to the original topic. Some of the students felt stifled by the inability to continue their dialog. The air was thick enough that they needed CPR to breathe. The overall mood was quite unsettling, as if a lit fuse was snaking its way to a tanker truck of nitroglycerin.

Pressure Cooker

Pressure was building up in me as well. I was perturbed by the professor for trying to lasso the free-flowing debate among intelligent adults. I felt she was uncomfortable with the topic, so she extinguished it like a two-alarm fire rather than encouraging them to draw it to a healthy conclusion. The professor's inflexibility really got me hot, and there was no putting out my flames.

I generally fight for the underdog and have righteous indignation on behalf of those controlled by anyone based on a position of political power, economic status, academic credentials, IQ, social stature, race, ethnicity, or Hollywood looks.

Bull in a China Shop

I had about as much as I could take. I then tore through the discussion, gathering up my belongings while blurting out something about not standing for this bullshit anymore, and stormed out of the classroom, making a beeline for my car.

Perfect Storm

What drove me to react in that fashion? I believe it was the stress of work, taking two night classes a term, working full time, co-parenting two young children, studying harder to compensate for my cognitive disabilities, and irregular sleeping patterns. It was a perfect storm for a manic episode.

Messed-Up Brain Chemistry

To say I was upset was an understatement. I was out of control, acting on sheer adrenaline and messed-up brain chemistry. I was confident all the way home that night that I'd taken a brave stance in supporting freedom of speech, the underprivileged, and under-appreciated. I was their standard-bearer, their self-appointed Joan of Arc! Until the next day, when I woke up. Thinking about the night before, I wasn't sure if I'd had a dream or was currently in one.

Reality is sometimes hard to discern in the transition from mania to depression. It was then I realized that I had outed my bipolar behavior and exposed the me that was previously unknown by my fellow grad students and professor. I think that up to then, I generally came across as an outgoing, intelligent, and creative individual who was passionate about the education he was receiving.

Now, I thought they saw me as a nut.

What to Do?

What should I do? Drop out? Presume nothing happened? Tell everyone it was my evil twin? To my relief and appreciation, my fellow grad students were very accepting and understanding. I had the feeling, however, that my professor may have had a different take on the issue. So, I did what I felt most appropriate: I made an appointment to see my professor and beg for forgiveness.

We made an appointment for later that week. It took place in her cloistered office, with barely enough room for her, me, and the surprise presence of the department head. The chairs were close, and so was the air. You could have cut it with a knife. My professor sliced through the silence like a boxcutter, declaring the beginning of the discussion.

Blazing Mania

When you are ablaze with mania, your mind and body are in synchronous heat, enough to melt through traditional wisdom and appropriate behavior. The intensity can go beyond yourself and badly singe once close social relationships and burn long-standing bridges beyond recognition.

Dazed and Confused

When I was unexpectedly outed by my graduate school manic episode, I realized the jig was up. Time to admit to the world I was bipolar. But having survived and even thrived after letting people know I have bipolar disorder, the only confusion that remains is why did I resist coming out for so long? Stigma: I have found the only way to overcome it is to embrace it.

It was a pretty simple, straightforward inquisition. I handed my explanation to them on a silver platter, no hemming or hawing, no excuses or alibis. I had overreacted, I was inappropriate, I disrupted the class, and I have bipolar disorder.

Unprepared

I was expecting their jaws to drop, but instead, they said, "Oh, we figured that." Huh, what was that you said? I thought. Instead, I asked in a matter-of-fact way how they knew. They answered, "Oh, we could tell for a long time."

So, I'd been sized up long ago—and made a topic of conspiratorial conversation. Silly me, thinking I could pass for "normal." But I was unprepared for coming out—especially for discovering that I'd already been outed without knowing it.

I gave my word that from then on, I would try to control myself and act civilly. Upon everyone agreeing that it had been good to talk, I subserviently stepped out of the office with my tail between my legs, reminiscent of being caught with one's hand in the cookie jar. Except I wasn't caught with a cookie.

I was caught with a whole new identity and forced to face the music of being known as someone with a mental disorder, at which point... I crumbled.

Poem

I was left with such raw feelings

I've never felt like that before

Humiliation, confusion

I felt like hiding from the world

I could have used an attic then

I had to process what happened

I had to rid it out of me

A demon hiding in myself

Not where it was supposed to be

I knew I had to set it free

I delved inside my feeble brain

To grab that scary entity

It was out and became my art

I was left with such raw feelings

Questions

Do you have a diagnosis you kept to yourself that became exposed in a social setting? If so, how did others respond when it was exposed?

What was more surprising, your demonstration of behavior or their response to you? Why?

What could have been the bipolar student's more constructive response to the professor and administrator? Do you think there could have been a more constructive response? Why or why not?

How do you draw the line between righteous indignation and an inappropriate overreaction in protest? Can you justify either for the sake of advocacy or taking a moral stance against injustice? Why or why not?

Did the professor and administrator do an adequate job of discussing the situation? Why or why not?

CHAPTER 3

I Sensed My Artwork
Is Profound

Serendip
Bipolar Impaired Self
Cracked Window

The Bipolar Impaired Self

The pain of the Bipolar Impaired Self is more than excruciating. It is like a baby bunny, clamped between the muscle-bound jaws of a Rottweiler, being swung side to side until passing out or dying, or worse yet, left bleeding and barely alive.

"The position of the artist is humble. He is essentially a channel."

–Piet Mondrian

I had an impulse to share my images with the academic world; my newly-found discovery of my internal bipolar self turned outward. I spontaneously began looking up websites, seeking a home for my art. I wasn't sure where to look but feverishly flipped through website after website with search terms containing the words "bipolar," "creativity," and "artwork."

Serendip is a neurobiological website founded by the late neurobiologist Paul Grobstein, who was educated at Harvard University and chair of the biology department at Bryn Mawr College. Serendip is a unique education exchange platform that amazingly averages more than 20,000 unique visitors per day, with more than 99% off-campus. It is referred to as a "digital ecosystem" for exploration and a collaborative learning community in education, science, and the humanities.

Serendip is also the birthplace of my concept of the Bipolar Impaired Self. This communal, intellectual playground enabled me to discover the connection between my art, impairment, and the self.

Took a Chance

My quest for recognition and validation received a meaningful boost when I submitted samples of my artwork—along with an explanation of its connection to my lived experience with bipolar disorder—through the "contact us" link on Serendip. To my surprise and delight, my work immediately resonated with Professor Paul Grobstein, who invited me to contribute both my story and images to the site.

Since then, my work has found a permanent home on Serendip—an honor I hold with deep pride. I must add that Professor Grobstein struck a chord with me as well. A true embodiment of creativity and intellectual curiosity, he was the consummate academic and teacher, well-known for his distinctive style as a "scientific storyteller."

While exploring the website, I came across thoughtful and insightful comments linked to my artwork—left by students and visitors alike. Unbeknownst to me, Professor Grobstein had incorporated my images and narratives into a class assignment, encouraging students to interpret symbolic meaning and offer reflections. "Eye in Eye" is one such example. My accompanying narrative appears on the following page.

23

Patterns Emerged

To my amazement, patterns of both negative and positive self-characteristics began to emerge from the students' interpretations. Their insightful impressions offered more than just commentary—they served as data, illuminating a unique perspective on bipolar impairment. Their responses helped light a path toward deeper understanding of the inner world I would come to describe as the Bipolar Impaired Self.

Inspired, I returned to my own data—reigniting the flame that had, not long before, sparked the imaginations of a university professor and his students.

Birth of the Bipolar Impaired Self

Something powerful happened at the intersection of my artwork and the students' responses. Their insights didn't just analyze my images—they connected with something deep inside me. Together, we started an unexpected conversation about the self, filtered through the lens of bipolar stigma.

That's when the Bipolar Impaired Self began to take shape—not just as a concept, but as a reflection of the emotional and social weight I had carried for so long. It wasn't just about the ups and downs of my mood disorder. It was everything extra I had to face—judgment, misunderstanding, isolation.

Naming this impaired self—seeing it as something beside me instead of being me—changed everything. It gave form to what I could never quite explain before: the vague ache, the quiet struggle, the constant sense of something being off. For the first time, I had words for what had only been feelings.

Impaired Self—Cracked Window to the World

When I was a kid, I was a Little League catcher. I wouldn't say I liked it much. I had the impression that it was the position reserved for the fat kids who couldn't run fast—which, at the time, described me pretty well.

My dad, who probably thought the same thing deep down, still offered some sage advice. He told me that being a catcher was a privilege. In his ever-encouraging way, he said it was one of the most important roles on the field. The catcher may not get much attention, but he's part of every play.

I didn't really believe him back then—but years later, that idea helped me make sense of the self I write about in this book.

Like the catcher, the Bipolar Impaired Self often goes unnoticed, hidden behind the mask, crouched in the shadows, taking every pitch. It doesn't get the spotlight, but it's involved in every moment of the game. And just like my younger self behind the plate, it's easy to overlook how much effort it takes just to stay in the game, let alone play it well.

Eye in Eye

My 'inner eye' sees the world differently than does my outer eye. It's a different kind of observation and vision—more sensitive, intuitive, and perceptive. People see my outer eye and if they look closely enough, they may see my inner one as well. Then sometimes it's hard to tell the difference. —D Feingold

When any part of you is hidden or unacknowledged the whole self is limited in every way. Self-acceptance means not only acknowledging the less desirable parts but also allowing every aspect of the self to realize its true potential. —Submitted by A

Top: *Clear window of an unimpaired self*
Bottom: *Cracked window of the Impaired Self*

Clear Window

Imagine a sparkling clean window—so clear you don't even realize it's there. You simply see the world through it. The self is like that. Most of the time, we're unaware of it, quietly shaping how we experience life (Finlay, 2006).

Cracked Window

Now, picture a window with deep, jagged cracks. That's what the Impaired Self is like. Suddenly, you can't ignore the window. The cracks distort everything you see, interfering with your view—and your life.

This is the fallout of the Bipolar Impaired Self: the distortion, the disruption, the damage that makes everyday living harder. The more someone is burdened by bipolar stigma—and the fewer internal or external supports they have—the more those cracks spread. The wider they reach, the more life gets obscured.

When the glass finally shatters, the damage can be irreversible. Tragically, up to 20% of people with bipolar disorder die by suicide..

Poem

I sensed my artwork is profound
It showed what lived inside of me—
Like scars from stigma, pain, and shame
They said I wasn't "normal" then

They called me "crazy," wrote me off
I sensed my artwork is profound
But still, my art would speak for me
It gave me power over fear

The world deserved to see this truth—
What stigma really does to us
I sensed my artwork is profound
This is what they have made of me

Serendip posted what I drew
Students responded with insight
They saw beyond what others missed
I sensed my artwork is profound

Questions

Why do you think it is important for some individuals to share personal artistic expressions in response to a psychiatric crisis? What are some benefits to the artist? What are some drawbacks?

What role do you think artwork can play in communicating to people about the mental illness experience? What are some of the benefits, if any, to the viewer and to society?

The students who commented on the art images gave very thoughtful and rather objective interpretations. Do you think culture, age and education level help determine the attitude one has toward viewing a mental illness? Why or why not?

CHAPTER 4

Art Depicts All My True Feelings

Cracks in the Window
Stigma
Self-Stigma

Painful Tears

Painful tears are somewhat, well, painful to talk about. These tears aren't tears of joy or happiness. They are the despair of being in the bipolar moment, when one finds themself in a deep depression, a ruined relationship, a counterproductive action, and the awareness that they carry a destructive stigma. These tears become "tears" in the fabric of your soul.

"One eye sees, the other feels."

–*Paul* Klee

If anything cracks my window to the world, it's the collision of three forces that come with mental illness, including bipolar disorder: stigma, self-stigma, and passing.

Stigma

Lazowski et al. (2012) report that many people would rather distance themselves from someone with a mental illness as much as they would from a person with a drug dependency or a criminal record.

You may have seen the signs of the Impaired Self in others—or felt them in yourself: anger, self-loathing, rejection, humiliation, shame, poor self-image, fear, confusion, vulnerability, feeling exposed, worthlessness.

To live under the stigma of mental illness is to stand just this side of full humanity—balancing on a razor's edge, one misstep away from being cast into a sea of disgrace. A place where the "undeserving" are banished, far from the world where "normal" people live.

Self-Stigma

But it doesn't stop there. Not only must a person labeled "mentally ill" exist within the crushing boundaries society creates, they must also navigate the internalization of that mindset—a phenomenon known as self-stigma (Oral, 2007).

I remember my first encounter with self-stigma vividly. Although my memory is faulty due to a closed head injury in my teens, I'll never forget the moment my psychiatrist first told me I had bipolar disorder. I went numb—like I was outside my own body. I remember looking around the room, half expecting that the doctor was talking to someone behind me. But I was the only one there. It was me. I was the one with the abhorrent illness.

I Felt Half-Baked

After that, I couldn't process anything the doctor said. A haze of confusion and disbelief took over. My sense of identity dissolved.

I felt like a grade 2 potato in a world where only grade 1s were allowed in fine restaurants. Worse than that—I felt half-baked. Half a person. Half-alive.

Like a teenager with arrested development, unsure of my place or status in a world unmarked by bipolar disorder. Adulthood felt skewed from that point on.

My self-esteem and self-efficacy dropped to near zero. I couldn't trust my own judgment—because I was now a "mentally ill" person. A pariah to others—and to myself. Society's stigma, prejudice, and harsh judgment ran through my veins. I could no more remove them than a zebra could its stripes.

How Does Self-Stigma Happen?

How do spirit and positive thinking slowly dissolve in the face of stigma?

Have you ever noticed how, if people repeat something often enough, you start to believe it—even if you didn't at first? Political propaganda comes to mind. The same process occurs when one internalizes society's relentless barrage of stereotypes, prejudice, and misinformation about mental illness. Over time, their view becomes your view. Their judgment becomes your voice.

Look no further than the media for examples. But this time, we choke on what they feed us. Popular movies, news broadcasts, and headlines serve up a steady diet of distortion and fear.

Research shows that the vast majority of media coverage about mental illness focuses on violence. In fact, up to 75 percent of articles on the topic frame individuals with mental illness as dangerous (Corrigan et al., 2005).

Watson et al. (2007) identified common stereotypes: people with mental illness are seen as incompetent, dangerous, and to blame for their own condition. The irony is devastating. These very beliefs—intended to isolate and condemn—are known contributors to depression (Crocker, 2002) and identity loss (Michalak, Yatham, Kolesar, & Lam, 2006) in those who are already vulnerable.

Passing

In my own life, there are moments when I feel strong, assertive—able to speak up and claim my space. But then, almost like an echo, comes the voice inside: You're flawed. You're subnormal. You don't deserve the same respect or treatment as others.

To protect myself from judgment and social rejection, I often hide my illness. I withdraw, isolate, and avoid interactions where my bipolar disorder might be revealed. This strategy—this act of passing—feels like survival. But it's also erasure. I disappear to remain acceptable.

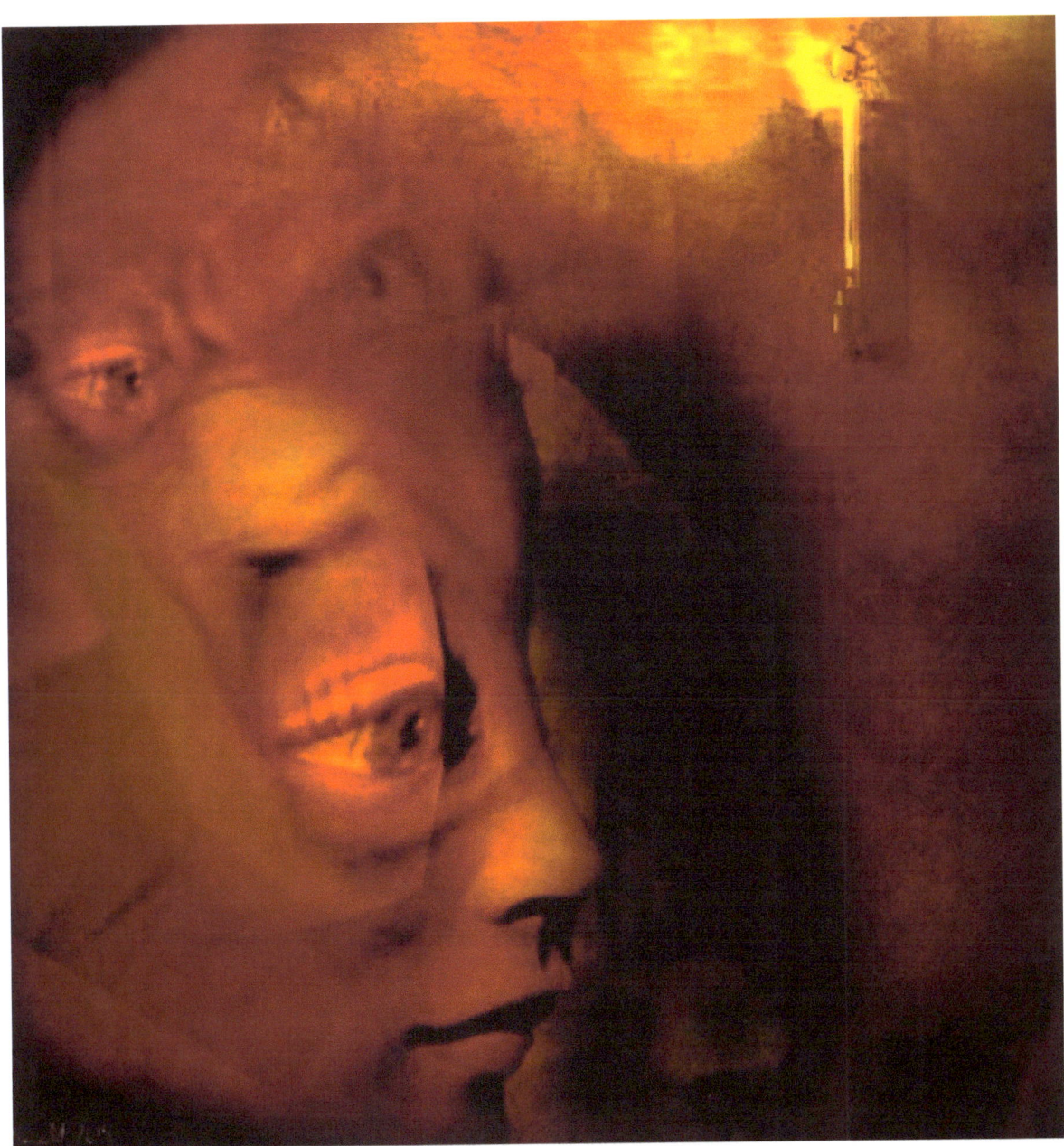

Self-Stigma

When something is attributed to you, you get it in your head that it must be true. When assaulted with stigmatizing insults and constantly identified as a lower life form, it seeps into your consciousness. It eats away at your self-esteem and identity like wood rot. What crawls out of that Bipolar Impaired Self is fear, helplessness, doubt, and sorrow.

Lying Through My Teeth
Through my blocked teeth, more like it. Keeping my diagnosis to myself paints a picture of deception. However, it is also a shield that deflects painful negative stereotypes, bias, and stigma lobbed at you by insensitive and misinformed individuals. It most often results in feeling angry and humiliated. It's not only cringe-worthy but worthy of you being deceptive.

The complexity and chronic stress involved in managing public disclosure—what Goffman referred to as "passing" (Watson & Helou, 2006)—means hiding what is perceived as a defective or "spoiled" identity. This effort increases self-consciousness and emotional strain, requiring constant scanning of the social landscape to protect one's identity, reputation, and psychological well-being (Beals, Peplau & Gable, 2009).

Close to the Vest

I've never been a good liar. I'm too naive to see the benefit of twisting the truth, too transparent to hide it, and too cognitively impaired to remember it.

And yet—I might lie through my teeth around people who don't know me well. Why? Because I carry a secret. A secret that, if revealed at the wrong time or to the wrong person, could lead to anything from awkward silence to outright disaster.

Research consistently shows that people with bipolar disorder are often viewed as dangerous (Angermeyer & Matschinger, 2003). The label of "dangerousness" isn't just a stereotype—it's situational. It determines who is trusted, who is hired, and who is deemed "fit" for certain roles.

For example, I genuinely believe that if the staff or parents at the school where I worked had known I had bipolar disorder, they might have second-guessed whether their children should be referred to me at all.

Similarly, it's hard to imagine a person with a known bipolar diagnosis being appointed CEO of a Fortune 500 company—especially one that manufactures war machines.

And no one is likely to offer someone like me a volunteer position as the sole adult leading children on a remote overnight wilderness trip.

The discomfort, guilt, and anxiety of needing to conceal one's condition—to be less than fully honest just to be seen as acceptable—feeds directly into the development of an Impaired Self.

To me, hiding one's bipolar disorder isn't just a form of self-protection. It's a learned survival strategy, born from public shaming, discrimination, isolation, and exclusion (Byrne, 2000).

But it comes at a cost. It feels like deception—not just of others, but of who I truly am.

Open Wounds

I've found that, despite the personal growth and hard-won adaptations I've made since first showing symptoms of bipolar disorder, the difficulties aren't just remnants of a distant diagnosis.

They're ever-present forces—waiting in the wings, ready to resurface and shake my sense of self and safety. They're not like cuts you treat with antibiotic salve, then bandage and forget. These are open wounds. No first aid kit can close them for good—and neither can the passage of time.

Emotional Scars

Just as visible external scars mark the site of a physical injury or illness, my art—drawn from deep within—is a collection of virtual scars.

Each image reflects the inner, psycho-emotional wounds that often accompany mental health impairments and disabilities, including bipolar disorder.

Ravaged

It's easy to feel ravaged by this illness. You are either facing a damaging bipolar-related dilemma, remembering one, or anticipating the next. It may or may not be at the surface level of consciousness, but the seed that had been planted long ago continues to germinate in the rocky soil of poor brain chemistry. You feel ravaged, trapped in its twisted roots.

Poem

Art depicts all my true feelings

Art reveals society's gaze

Art reflects my spoiled identity

Art displays my innermost scars

Constant struggling impairs my self

Embarrassment and shame cut deep

I make mistakes and have faux pas

People judge and even sneer

Lack trust in my abilities

And then they infantilize me

The worst part of being bipolar

People praise me for being brave

And then I see them turn away

Art depicts all my true feelings

Questions

Stigma occurs when society denigrates people with impairments and disabilities. Stigma adds a whole other layer of challenges when dealing with an impairment or disability. How do you think it affects the person? What types of additional challenges do they create?

Do you think there are ways to inoculate oneself or diminish the Impaired Self's effects on an individual? In what ways and to what extent?

Passing as someone without a mental illness can protect yet also obscure one's identity. Can these two effects reconcile and justify the practice of passing? If so, in what way(s)? If not, why not?

CHAPTER 5

I Was Impaired
By Accident

Inner Significance Of My Art
Hit-And-Run Accident
Cognitive Confusion

Bad Karma

Bad karma refers to getting struck down by a car as a pedestrian when I was 16 years of age. Crossing the street with a close friend of mine landed me on the pavement, which landed me in an ambulance, which landed me in the hospital. Years later, a neurologist told me that the traumatic brain injury, landed me my temporal lobe epilepsy and my bipolar disorder. Who would have guessed that crossing the street could take me to so many places, especially considering I never made it to the other side.

"There is no such thing as accident; it is fate misnamed."

–Napoleon Bonaparte

It was a steamy summer night in Chicago, 1967. But humidity wasn't the only thing hanging in the air. I remember an eerie stillness—an impending doom. It felt like the chilling déjà vu that sometimes follows an absence seizure.

Strangely, at the time, I thought that ominous feeling came from my decision to stop at the 7-Eleven with a friend. In my family, I was required to bring home milk after a night out. Not having milk in the fridge was seen as a nutritional emergency—my parents feared malnourishment and vitamin D deficiency as being a familial disaster.

Still, I often got scolded for going to 7-Eleven instead of the regular grocery store. They didn't appreciate me paying extra for milk while standing in line behind a guy in a ski mask preparing for a holdup.

But on that particular night, karma had something else in store. I never made it across the street. The next morning, I woke up disoriented and confused. A nurse checking my vitals informed me I'd been in a hit-and-run. According to my friend, I had flown through the air after being struck, and landed headfirst on the pavement along Devon Avenue.

Left for Dead

It turned out that going to the 7-Eleven cost me more than the proverbial arm and leg. It wound up costing me my head, specifically the amygdala on the right side of my brain. A closed head injury developed scar tissue in that area, which led to temporal lobe epilepsy.

I would find, as I aged, that neurological trauma would lead to significant cognitive and emotional impairments and disabilities in the form of memory loss, forgetfulness, and general disorganization.

I now deal with this on a daily basis. Sometimes I find myself thinking about the driver. His brakes screeching to a halt, and his head darting out the open car window, craning to see what damage might have befallen the person once standing.

He may have sped away, as my friend described, "Like a bat out of hell," yet my conclusion always remains the same. Not knowing whether he had just committed vehicular manslaughter and left me for dead, the direction he faced was undoubtedly not away from hell but toward it.

Grade School in the Twilight Zone

Bits and pieces of my life are suspended like a colloidal solution in a mason jar. I can glance at one memory floating there, and if I want to see another, I simply give the jar a shake or a swirl.

Just as the hit-and-run accident is one of those fragments, so too is my life as a student. Even before the accident, I was never what you'd call a great student. I mostly earned Cs and Bs—with more than a few Ds sprinkled in. Looking back, I'm fairly certain I had undiagnosed learning differences. No matter how hard I tried, I couldn't keep up. The teachers and students always seemed two steps ahead, while I was still trying to make sense of what had just been said or written on the board.

No extra help from teachers, no tutoring from family, no guidance from friends made much difference. My brain didn't work like everyone else's. Every school day felt like slow-motion torture. Schoolwork, homework, oral reports, and pop quizzes weren't just academic tasks—they were daily reminders of inadequacy.

Rod Serling couldn't have written a better script for my grade school experience. It wasn't a cheerful neighborhood schoolhouse. It was a psychological haunted house—every hallway echoing with dread.

After the hit-and-run accident and resulting closed head injury, new challenges crept in, stealthy and cruel. Each school day became another episode in a personal terror anthology—one where I was both the hunter and the hunted.

Devon Avenue had used my head as a bowling ball, and from that moment on, my ability to be a "good" student only worsened. As the schoolwork grew more abstract and disconnected from my interests, my sense of competence collapsed.

I developed coping mechanisms that were more theatrical than helpful—like trying to calm Frankenstein with stand-up comedy. I used crib notes on test days and claimed my dog ate my homework, though even that excuse felt more honest than my feeble attempts to succeed.

School felt like a prison. Apathy from teachers locked the door, and the cognitive impairments from my head injury threw away the key. I was slow to learn, quick to forget, hopeless at organizing, and incapable of staying on task.

But I didn't have a name for any of that back then. In my mind, I was just plain stupid.

These experiences—disabilities left untreated, confusion mistaken for laziness, and a growing sense of failure—began to shape something deeper and more insidious. The beginnings of what I would later come to understand as the Impaired Self.

My Tortured Student Soul
If you misbehave, you could find yourself "in detention." If you don't pass, you "fail."
If you fail too much, you'll be "held back." If you're held back, you can "flunk out."
Graduation isn't just an accomplishment; it's an escape route.

Fractured Past

Studying for tests wasn't easy in college because of my cognitive deficits. While others were burning the midnight oil, I was clueless, with my life in turmoil.

Confused in College

It didn't take long for me to realize that if my early education was difficult, then college would be no cakewalk.

Starting my freshman year at Southern Illinois University in Carbondale felt like being dropped into kindergarten all over again. I was that unprepared.

SIU wasn't an elite university, but I knew that any institution of higher learning would require more from me—academically, socially, and organizationally—than public education ever had. And that was already more than I could manage.

Beyond the coursework, I was constantly misplacing my student ID card (which I needed for meals), getting turned around trying to find my classes, and struggling to keep track of what day of the week it was.

To say I was a scatterbrain in college would be an understatement. These weren't quirky habits—they were symptoms of deeper cognitive impairments. But I didn't have that language yet.

It became part of my social persona: I was well-liked, creative, self-reflective, a little eccentric, immature. I stood out—but not always in ways that earned respect. My poor self-help and daily living skills made me seem unreliable or a flake. I was interesting, but not someone to be taken too seriously.

As the semesters went on, I didn't just feel like a scatterbrain. I began to feel like my brain was literally scattered.

I experienced strange episodes—moments when I would mentally drift away, like I was no longer in my body. A wave of déjà vu would hit me, followed by nausea, a sense of impending doom, and brief disorientation. The episodes came out of nowhere and lasted only seconds, but their aftershocks—mental fog, dizziness, and irregular breathing—could linger for hours.

I kept asking myself, What are these things?

Poem

I was impaired by accident
I always had trouble in school
I tried real hard to compensate
But I still fell short of good grades
My self-esteem was rock bottom
My identity was tarnished
I grew up thinking I was dumb

Things got worse for me in college
I kept losing and missing things
I would lose my way on campus
I started to feel out of it
It became quite disconcerting
I did not know what was wrong
I was impaired by accident

Questions

Knowing how accidents and serious illnesses can dramatically change the course of someone's life for the worse, it makes sense to appreciate what you have in the present. Has this ever happened to you or a loved one? How has it changed your or their lives? What can you do now to appreciate what you have?

Accidents can cause people to lose abilities they once had, which is an impairment. When an impairment interferes with performance, it is disabling. The person can then be said to have a disability. Have you ever been impaired by an acquired illness or accident? If so, what feeling states did you experience after first becoming impaired?

CHAPTER 6

I Was A Good Husband And Dad

My Family Was Everything
Developed Bipolar Disorder
Turmoil Begins

Flower Power

Spending time in our garden was a definite perk of home ownership. Summer was dotted and dappled with reds, yellows, and oranges, lightening the day and uplifting my spirits. And then, allergies. A divine pastime turned into a perverse curse.

"Without a family, man, alone in the world, trembles with the cold."

–Andre Maurois

I was the garden-variety family man—happy at home whether grilling in the backyard, installing shelves in the home office, or scooping dead leaves from the gutters in the fall.

I was a dedicated father, attending school orientations and holiday concerts, driving my daughter to and from playdates, and accompanying my son to guitar practice on Saturdays—followed by lunch at Tony's, a local sub shop. (Once, to my son's delight, I unconsciously poured iced tea over my sub, mistaking it for hot sauce.)

My family was my life, and our warm, extended families made a good thing even better. I had what I believed was everything I'd ever need: a loving family, a house, a job I liked, and good health.

Or so I thought.

Nothing to Sneeze At

It was springtime. The magnolia trees were celebrating the end of a frigid winter with their fragrant blossoms. Geese returned in V-formation, tracing the same skies they had flown south just months before.

Meanwhile, I was battling an intense case of allergies—something I had never experienced. In the past, I barely sneezed, even when surrounded by blooms in our backyard flower garden.

But this spring was different. I couldn't breathe through my nose at all, and my nasal drip ran like an open faucet. My general practitioner prescribed a cocktail of allergy medications: tablets, capsules, and nose sprays.

That medication regimen turned out to be a tragic double-edged sword. I would later learn from a neurologist that, for some people, high doses of allergy medications can trigger dormant bipolar disorder.

Only the Beginning

While still giddy over fooling Mother Nature with my potent array of prescriptive pharmaceuticals, I began to experience the sudden onset of emotions that were alien to my natural temperament. I would feel out of sorts, down, and hopeless for no apparent reason. Then, I faced crying spells, loss of confidence, and loss of interest in things that had previously brought me joy.

Everything—from doing my usual chores at home to being productive at work—became meaningless and overwhelming. Life began to feel like a life sentence, seemingly without parole.

I started to withdraw: as a husband and father at home, and as a co-worker at the school where I was on staff. It took everything in me just to remain somewhat lucid and present with my family and students.

I felt like I was walking in darkness, guided only by a flashlight with a dying battery—its beam dimming by the minute.

As the days passed, it became painfully clear that I was losing my grip. But where would I fall if I let go?

That's part of the terror built into this kind of illness. You don't know how far you'll fall—or where depression might take you. You don't know how it will manifest, or how it might devolve.

One thing is certain:

You, the actor, have changed.

The script is rewritten.

The plot is revamped.

This has become the new story of your life.
And you can't exchange stories, because…

There's No Librarian

Who do you ask for a different story when no one is around to ask? Simple. No one. You're stuck with the story that's been thrown at you. In fact you hurt from having the book thrown right between your eyes.

Before having this illness, you could anticipate what life might be like in the next few hours, days, and even weeks. With bipolar disorder, that type of thinking is presumptuous and unrealistic. You never know how you might manifest some of the characteristics, such as being profoundly depressed, anxious, impulsive, speaking inappropriately for the situation, having self-aggrandizing thoughts, pressured and run-on speech, having poor judgment, taking on responsibilities without following through or being sexually provocative.

It's like Russian Roulette. You never know which symptom is in the next chamber of the barrel. The plot thickened as my story continued to write itself. Yet all I wanted it to do was end. Far from ending, little did I know that the story was just beginning. I had yet to experience the manic phase of bipolar disorder. Even with the early depressive stages of bipolar disorder, I knew something was not quite right.

The Librarian Is Out

Librarians, especially school librarians, were always somewhat mysterious to me as a child. They seemed to like the books more than the students. So it is no surprise that I depicted the librarian in my book as needing a major makeover, just like my life.

Crossing the Line

Crossing the line in a relationship is a bridge too far. A bridge that leads you over the still waters of rationality, appropriateness, and commitment. But you wind up in a rushing whirlpool of temporary lust before being taken over by a permanent, turbulent state of misery and heartbreak. Oh, ye bipolar. You taketh us across the line, only to have us hang ourselves with it!

Not so with my manic phases of bipolar disorder. It was like a thousand suns had broken through the darkest cloud cover imaginable—the kind with the power to destroy life on Earth in sci-fi movies.

And why would anyone—after hours, days, or weeks of bone-deep depression—think there was something wrong with suddenly feeling good and rejuvenated?

But as the saying goes: if it sounds too good to be true, it is.

Crossing the Line

My manic phases would last days, and my less intense hypomanic phases, weeks (picture the difference between a sword and a knife: they differ in size but can both cut rather deeply). You cross impulsivity with hypersexuality and skewed judgment and have a perfect storm for self-destruction.

No matter how many years pass, it remains a raw and perpetual source of heartbreak in my life. Suffice it to say that I crossed the line, and it took me to a shadowy, horrific place known generally as divorce. It also meant I hurt my wife tremendously and likely stole her belief in trust. I no longer lived in our family home, unable to experience our children grow into teenagers and young adults. Visits aren't exactly the same as living together.

My transgressions caused me to miss half my life as a husband and father. It happened before I was on medication. In fact, it happened even before I knew I had bipolar disorder, even though I was displaying its symptoms. An excuse? Maybe. A fact? Definitely. Cross impulsivity with hypersexuality and skewed judgment, and you have a perfect storm for destruction. The concept of a future is entirely nonexistent when one is in the throes of mania.

The profound energy flowing through the body and mind seems to overshadow the power of karma, cause, and effect; as you sow, so shall you reap, what goes around comes around, and an eye for an eye and tooth for a tooth. It overwhelms your senses, credibility, intuition, and intellectual ability. It is an elixir of folly and an aphrodisiac of irrational behavior. You have no insight into your behavior because you have no life outside of the manic moment. You live for it and serve it until it abandons you in your human errors.

When you are in the thick of mania, there is a disorientation from your previous discernment between right and wrong and between what is helpful and hurtful to yourself and others.

You can understand this by comparing it with the spatial disorientation of a scuba diver underwater who loses track of direction with only seconds left before running out of oxygen or an airplane pilot who can't tell up from down while attempting to avoid crashing into a fast-approaching mountain peak.

The results of losing or maintaining one's personal bearings in the face of the most alluring of human temptations can make or break a relationship, friendship, trust, honor, devotion, security, and even one's life. It's irreversible, irretrievable, and opens only one way: inward.

Once you enter, you never come out, at least not the same as when you walked in. Given the negative way you feel about yourself and how other people who knew you "when" avoid you now, you're hardly the same person.

There are times when you wake up from this nightmare only to realize you're still in it, but now with clarity. In my case, somewhere between mania and depression, the reality of my behavior broke through the haze I had been living with more remorse, guilt, and shame than I could handle.

I crumbled to a heap on the floor, a lone island encircled by a flood of my own tears, confessing the unthinkable for a garden-variety family man. Another ambulance ride to the hospital ER ensued. Last time for being hit by a car. This time, for being hit by reality.

Out of the Picture
Bipolar disorder affects more than just the afflicted. It affects the entire family. In my case, it changed the course of our lives and my role as a father, husband, and friend. I am literally "out of the picture." I can't be found in any pictures of my family and extended family. Walking out of the picture is bad enough, but the walking never ends.

Poem

I was a good husband and dad
And then bipolar disorder
I became very short-tempered
I distanced myself from loved ones
Transgressions took them all away
I've always missed my family
I'm not sure who I've become

Bipolar changed the course of time
My children did not deserve it
My family suffered greatly
It's been said that time heals all wounds
But what if they keep opening?
A never-ending tragedy
I was a good husband and dad

Questions

Have you ever experienced a situation where someone's usual positive behavior has unpredictably turned negative? What were the circumstances? How was the person behaving, and did others respond?

Depression can have severe effects on one's life. List three ways that depression can have a negative effect on one's personal life, family life, and employment.

What do you think is the worst part of having a manic episode? Why might it be difficult for people to be in the company of someone in a manic state?

CHAPTER 7

I Was Given Asylum

Even More Bipolar
Psych Ward
The Wait Escape

Insane Asylum

What a terrible name. Yet, those were places that "warehoused" mentally ill people at an earlier period in our history. There aren't functioning insane asylums anymore, at least not in the United States, other than the abandoned buildings themselves, seen as architectural and societal curiosities. However, the stigma related to those insane asylums remains in society and is internalized in our psyche. It has the effect of stunting our emotional and intellectual growth and leaving us feeling as powerless as a child in a straitjacket.

"I love bipolar people."

–Leon Russell

I was strapped to a stretcher—lifted up like a sacrifice to the gods of spiritually fallen husbands and fathers—and carried out of our house, feet first, to the waiting ambulance.

Men in uniforms hovered over me, talking into a crackling radio, checking my vitals, and trying to find a vein for the saline drip. The needle they used felt the size of a telephone pole.

A couple of tries came up empty. Then another medic took the syringe and went in for the kill. This guy was a pro.

I distinctly remember feeling the sleek, thick shaft of the needle sliding deep into the back of my hand—the sharp, burning pain welcoming me back to the world of the living.

The blaring sirens drowned out both my thoughts and the questions being flung at me like clay pigeons. Eventually, I managed to understand one and eked out my name and date of birth in rote monotone, as if speaking through an auxiliary voice apparatus.

The ambulance snaked through the streets of Highland Park like a steel ball in a labyrinth game, gaining speed as we neared the ER. The crew held onto railings to keep from crashing into equipment—or each other.

There were several of us in the ambulance, yet I felt utterly alone... though not as vulnerable as I did when I was with my family.

Little did I know then, that's how I would live the rest of my life—alone. We screeched to a halt. The back door swung open with surgical speed. Everything felt otherworldly. I saw myself not as a patient, but as a hitchhiker.

I wasn't bleeding. I hadn't been hit by anything. No broken bones. No lockjaw. I was whisked into the bowels of the ER, where figures in white coats and blue scrubs darted around under strobe-like fluorescent lights. Makeshift rooms were sectioned off by curtains, filled with people enduring visible, tangible pain.

It was chaotic. Impersonal. But efficient. A wristband with your name and a brisk introduction from a nurse or PA is all it takes to transform you from a nameless human to a patient.

As for me, I was wheeled into an 8x8-foot room—walls bare, fluorescent light overhead, a heavy wooden door behind me, and a window looking in. That window wasn't for me to see out.

Outside stood a uniformed guard, his job clear: Make sure I didn't try to escape, string myself up with the bedsheets, or smash my head against the wall until I passed out—or died.

But I didn't do any of those things. I just lay there, staring at the four blank walls. And sometimes, at the guard. Who occasionally looked up and stared back.

I sat there for hours before anyone came to talk with me. A few perfunctory questions were asked, then it was back to the ambulance—off to another hospital better equipped to handle my kind of problem, whatever that was.

This ambulance ride was different from the one after I'd been mowed down by a car. This time, I was lucid. I knew where I was and what was happening.

But was I a patient or a prisoner? I couldn't tell.

Inner Sanctum: The Psych Ward

Ever since I went on disability and stopped working, my concept of routine faded into oblivion—and stayed there. I live by the seat of my pants now: creating art when I feel like it, eating meals whenever, and falling asleep at who-knows-what-o'clock.

Not so in the psych ward. There, everyone wakes up at a specific time. That freedom is taken away. When it's time for meals, you eat whatever they give you. That freedom is taken away. You wear hospital garb. That freedom is taken away. Bedtime is not a suggestion. That freedom is taken away.

What if I'm not tired? What if I'm in the middle of journaling? It doesn't matter. Lights out.

The Joke's on You

I just came up with a hospital joke: "What's the difference between being locked up in a prison ward and being locked up in a psych ward?" "I don't know... but I'll tell you when I figure it out."

Hmmm. It's not funny, is it? Well, neither is being in a psych ward. You're surrounded by people who may be more deeply unwell than you. You're singled out as someone who needs special "treatment" from the rest of society. You're reduced to a diagnostic label.

As a former licensed clinical social worker, I know psychiatric hospitalizations can be necessary. I believe that. But let's be honest: it's not a pleasant experience.

"Hi, my name is Buddy. I'm a schizophrenic. What are you? How many times have you tried to kill yourself?" "Only once?" "Wow. Amateur."

It makes you feel like an underachiever.

Power Déjà Vu

I've seen the psych ward scenario before—the power relationship between the staff and the patients. It's reminiscent of our schools. As a staff member, I witnessed how

Let Me Out!

"Lights out" was the last thing I heard at night during my psychiatric hospitalizations. It was time to stop what you were doing and go to bed. Then, it was time for group therapy. Then it was time for arts and crafts. Then, it was time for lunch. Then it was time to talk with the psychiatrist. Then it was time for "free" time. In thinking about it, I find it interesting that macramé was never offered as an arts and crafts activity.

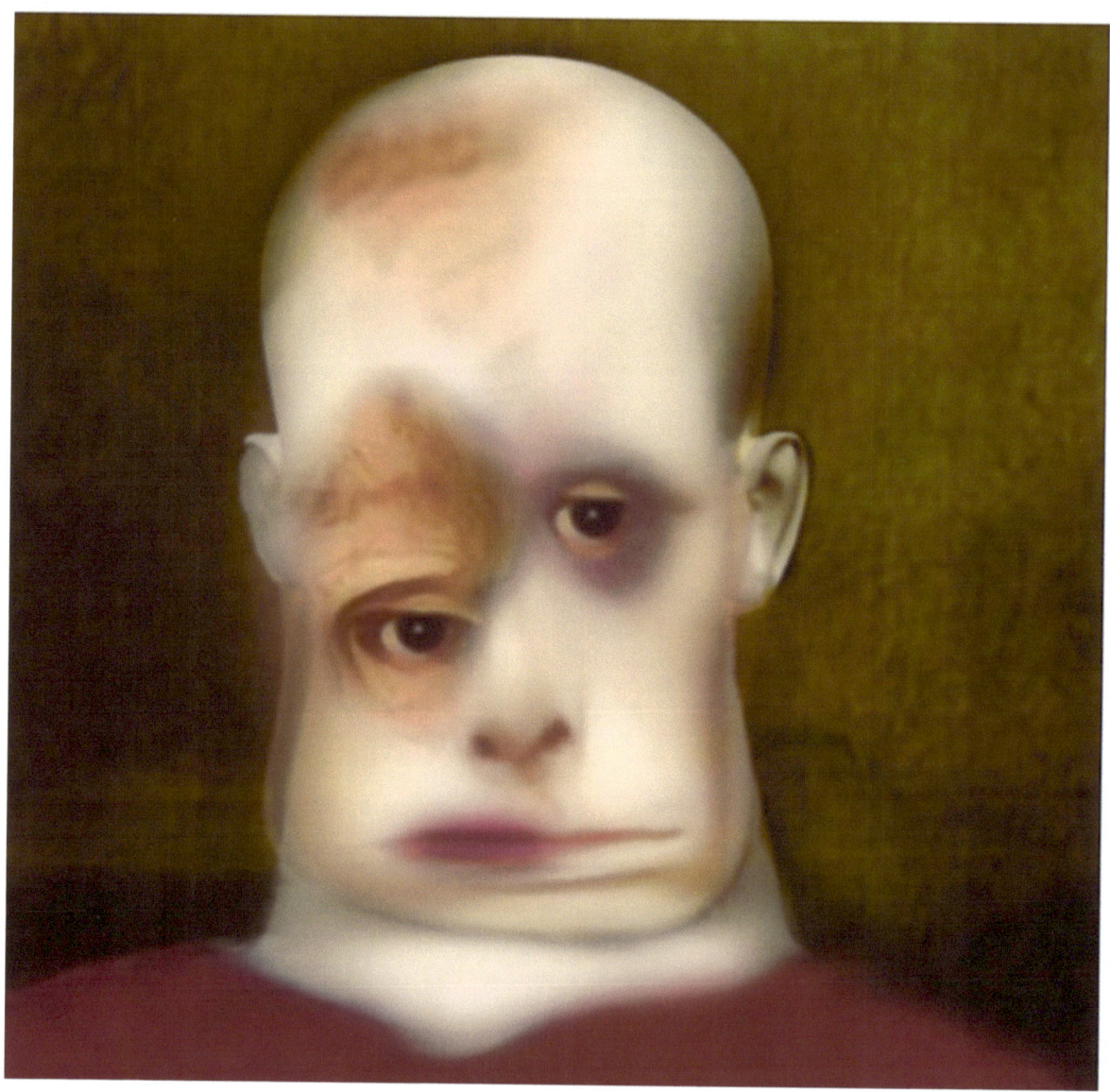

Being Insane Has Never Been "In"

It is a versatile word, however. It could mean extremely good or extremely bad. However, being considered insane is rarely a good thing. There used to be carnival slide shows called "freak shows." People with physical derivations from the norm were presented as curiosities for the entertainment of their patrons. What can be more insane?

the more complacent and compliant our students are with teachers, and teachers are with administrators, and administrators are with the superintendent, the superintendent is with the board, and the board is with the community; the more one gets what they want and avoids what they don't like. It's playing the game, working the system, being one step ahead of the person above you. It's being crazy—like a fox!

It's Time

My favorite part of being hospitalized for just under a week? Five-minute daily check-ins with the psychiatrists.

Five minutes. That's all the time they had to get to know me, assess my situation, and adjust my meds. That's where the real magic happened.

But the most memorable moment came a few days in—after I'd followed every instruction to the letter. "So," one of them asked, "do you think you're ready to go home now?" I was stunned. It was the first time in days anyone had asked me to make a decision—any decision.

It felt like not being trusted to drive a used Chevy Cobalt, then suddenly being handed the keys to a Learjet.

Was I ready? You tell me. What metric are you using? What chart are you checking? Oh right—whatever the insurance company defines as the "optimal length of inpatient stay."

So, after several days of group therapy, micro-sessions with psychiatrists, arts and crafts, mild stretching exercises, and mingling with some of the most fascinatingly unique people I've ever met.

It was time to go home. I was relaxed, no longer in acute crisis—and no longer practicing how to tie nooses.

Don't Question Our Responsibility

In retrospect, I think about the jokes that are often made about people being committed to a psych ward, to the "funny farm," "loony bin," or "mad house."

If outsiders who make light of these experiences could feel the pain and distress associated with psychiatric illness placements in a locked ward for one minute, we could have less ridicule, more empathy, less teasing, and more understanding.

Dr. Greendale a True Mentor

After my psychiatric hospitalization, I needed a psychiatrist who could manage my medication, provide therapeutic support, and evaluate my progress toward something resembling premorbid functioning.

I was fortunate to meet Dr. Greendale. Aside from being extraordinarily insightful and deeply knowledgeable, he did something rare: he listened carefully. When I described symptoms I believed were panic attacks, he referred me to a neurologist. He told me that panic attacks and seizures can present similarly—and, based on his assessment, mine resembled the latter.

Sure enough, the neurologist diagnosed me with temporal lobe epilepsy. To my chagrin, I learned that every seizure I'd had over the years had been quietly deep-sixing brain cells.

But here's the upshot: With Dr. Greendale's consistent support, I went from a barely functioning amoeba slumped in a patient chair to someone who could work again, enjoy life again—and even return to school to pursue a doctorate in Disability Studies.

Without this lover of symphony music, world travel, and fine photography— whose large-scale prints of distant lands decorated the walls of his office—I might have evolved from an amoeba to a paramecium, but certainly not to a doctoral student.

I've come a long way since first manifesting bipolar symptoms—including the spontaneous purchase of a motorcycle, dyeing my hair blonde, and sporting a dangling earring.

Decades later, I still feel the ache from that first ride off into the manic sunset, which ultimately ended in the foreshortened cliff of a dissolved marriage.

I've been able to build a reasonably good life since then. But the pain of that first fall from grace never completely leaves.

And likely never will.

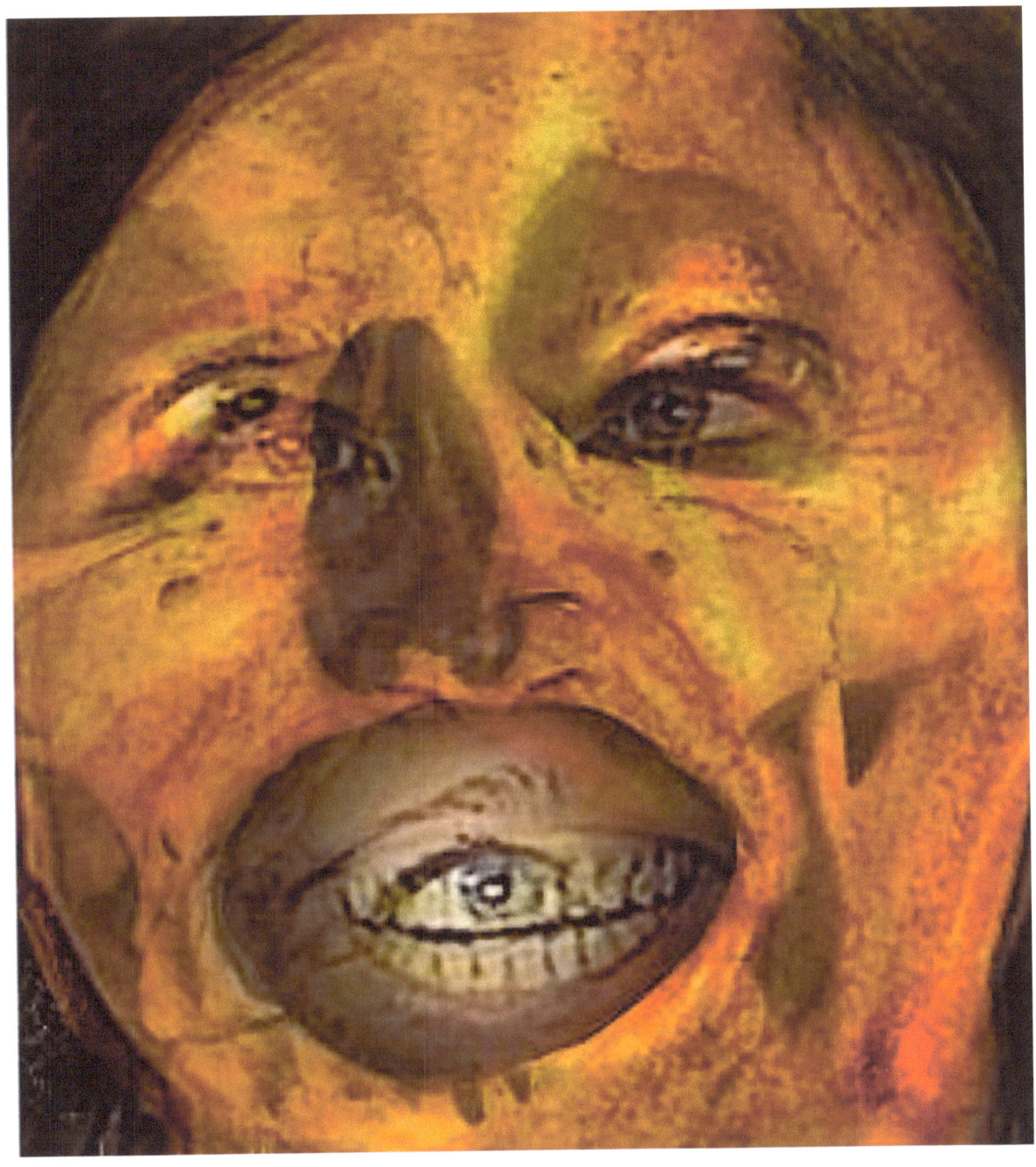

Ready to go Home?
So, when I was hospitalized, the psychiatrist asked if I was ready to go home. I deferred to him, and in the blink of an eye, he said, "Yes."

Poem

I was given asylum
I was no longer in control
I wondered what happened to me
An alien overtook me
Like a bull in a china shop
I was bucking the social rules
The whole time I was unaware

Being awake for days on end
Crossing the line and spending sprees
I didn't know what was happening
And then it struck me all at once
Something was really wrong with me
I found myself in a psych ward
I was given asylum

Questions

How might limiting the freedom and control of someone experiencing a psychological decompensation with hospitalization be helpful? Can it be counterproductive? If so, how?

What are some situations that can have adverse effects on someone's psychiatric hospitalization? What are some situations and conditions that can have positive influences? Why?

Psychiatric disorders can have significant negative effects on family members. Do you think there could be some positive outcomes for a family? What might they be, and how could they be achieved?

CHAPTER 8

My Family
Always Mattered

It's All Relative
I Quit
Just Getting By

All in the Family

Somewhere between "now" and "then" lie memories. Now, when separated from family, except for visits and then, a connection to the lives of people who made each day worth living. The memories before bipolar are ever-present, waiting for me to tap into them whenever I want to revisit those idyllic times. My children are adults now, and most of my memories are of them when they were young, and so was I. But while I was enjoying "the good life," I often wondered how unfair it was and how difficult it must be to live with major disabilities like total paralysis or severe cosmetic disfigurement, due to no fault of their own. And now, I know.

"Family is not an important thing. It's everything."

–Michael J. Fox

So what's it like for the family of someone with bipolar disorder? I suppose you'd have to ask them—but short of that, in my experience, people respond in very different ways.

Take my ex-wife. She found it difficult to talk about my bipolar disorder in any detail. I believe her silence had less to do with the condition itself and more to do with the pain caused by my marital infidelity—its impact on her, her family, and our mutual friends. That betrayal was real, and so were the wounds it left behind.

Let me be clear: although untreated bipolar disorder can sometimes be associated with impulsive decisions, including infidelity, it's all too easy to use the illness as a smoke screen to avoid facing the real issues in a relationship. No scapegoating here. Relationship problems are complex and require both partners to humbly take responsibility. Often, these issues begin long before a bipolar diagnosis is ever made.

Still, healing is possible. Post-divorce reconciliation—even if just emotional or symbolic—is crucial if family members hope to move forward without being forever defined by the past. The children deserve nothing less.

The good news? We both survived. Not just the illness, but the breakup. And in many ways, my ex-wife thrived. She chose to leave the weight of our shared pain behind and build a promising new life. Since our divorce, she has devoted herself to self-growth, spiritual exploration, deepening friendships, travel, professional reinvention, and preparing exquisite cuisine. She didn't let the past define her future.

I include her story not just out of respect, but to offer hope to those who have been hurt by their bipolar partners. After the pain, there is potential for a better life bathed in light on the other side of darkness.

Raising a Daughter Who Raises Spirits

My adult daughter has become more empathic, if not sympathetic. She checks on me regularly by phone from across the country. She always encourages me to take good physical care, get a social life, become more positive, and exercise.

She means well and never seems to give up on me. Seeing your father miss out on so much of what life has to offer can't be easy. One such situation occurred when I was having a detached emotional seizure response. It was in reaction to me feeling hurt that something my ex-wife said to me. My daughter (then in her early 20s) called for an ambulance and had me taken to the emergency room.

As she cradled my head in her arms, waiting for the ambulance to arrive through the white fog and diffused light, I heard her say, "I love you, Daddy." When she was a little girl, I used to be her guiding light. Now, I feel I'm barely a flicker in the night.

Boys to Men

I never thought to ask my son what it was like to have a father with bipolar disorder. Being ten years younger than his sister, he has never really known what life without a bipolar father is like. I was diagnosed when he was five. He's now in his early 30s. He's not one to share his emotions, though he's verbal and loves to talk—just not about this. Bipolar disorder isn't on his list of favorite topics.

He has seen me in major depressions. He's witnessed me speak inappropriately—saying unsavory things about people, making sexual innuendos in mixed company, acting cut off from the family. Looking back, some of what I expected him to process wasn't fair. That wasn't his burden to carry.

As a child, he was close to me. But like many teens, that shifted in adolescence—when spending time with a parent becomes more of an obligation than a celebration

Still, he was deeply challenged by having a bipolar father. I remember one moment clearly. His mother and I had argued over who would pay the co-pay for one of his doctor's visits. The argument left me despondent, hollow, scraped raw—as if something inside me had been peeled away with a potato peeler, over and over. There was nowhere to turn, no cave to enter and lick my wounds.

In broad daylight, I was sitting in the car with him beside me. I pulled over, shut off the ignition, and began to weep. A wave of pain rose from my toes to the top of my head. Tears streamed out of a shell who used to be me.

My Little Man

Without panic, without hesitation, my son calmly called 911—just as his sister had done years earlier.

When the paramedics arrived, they tried to gently pry my hands from the steering wheel. But I held on tight.

"I love my boy!" I screamed. "Don't take me away from my boy! Please—don't take me from my boy!"

Daddy's Girl
When a father and daughter who love each other to the very core of their DNA look into each other's eyes, they peer through them directly into the soul. At that point, you see not only the other's soul but your own.

My Guy
Fortunate are those children who have parents to admire them and those parents who are, in turn, admired by their children. It helps build a strong fortification against stressors and calamities. There's nothing like mutual "ad-mire-ation" to help face every "mire" in life.

When Madness Has A Witness

My son rode in front of the ambulance while I was being restrained in the back. This time, I was both manic and depressed. On the inside, I was utterly vacant—but from my mouth, the gateway from absolute lifelessness to the world outside, came blood-curdling screams of hysteria.

A mixed state of mania and depression is its own form of terror. It creates a psychic disconnect that tears the self in two, leaving behind a single identity: madness.

My son walked into the emergency room with me, never showing any outward signs of panic, fear, or confusion. He waited beside me, faithful to his duties as a son, until his mother arrived. She called for him from the outer waiting room.

I suppose what had just occurred only reinforced in her mind why she needed to maintain strict emotional boundaries. In addition to harboring resentment, I believe she needed to protect herself from the demons that had taken up residence in the stranger she once called her soulmate.

Family Affair

The picture on the following spread is of my brother, sister, our family dog, and me. I was the baby then.

Being the youngest came with both benefits and burdens. I was coddled, but also picked on—sounds sort of bipolar, doesn't it?

Despite the miles, my siblings and I kept a familial kind of attachment into adulthood. But our adult lives didn't include weekends spent at each other's homes, barbecues, or shared holidays. We lived scattered across the country, and though we cared, we lived from afar.

I never chased the so-called "better life" elsewhere. I stayed in Chicago. The rest of my family picked up stakes and didn't look back. At the time, I had my own young family—my wife and children—to help absorb the sorrow of being left behind.

But when I lost that family, too—when bipolar disorder took its toll—the absence of my family of origin became more than just emotional. It became existential. Their love remained, but from afar. And from a distance, there's only so much anyone can do.

A local, close-knit support system might have made those years pass more gently. But whatever karma placed me here seems to have written in a script of solitude: a life of deep love, brief relationships, and long stretches of silence. Most of my serious relationships with women lasted anywhere from one to eight years.

Still, I remained. Perhaps because somewhere beneath it all, I believed in return.

There's Never a Great Date to Make a Date

Being on a dating site with bipolar disorder is like whitewater rafting without a paddle. One way or another, you're going to get hurt. Either you hit your head on the rocks—or the rocks are already in your head for even trying.

Tell someone right away that you have bipolar disorder, and they're history. Wait until after you meet, and you're a scoundrel—accused of hiding something.

But there were exceptions. A few women I met—especially those who had their own health challenges—offered something different. I sensed their quiet resilience. They understood adversity from the inside. They didn't flinch. They didn't pity. They listened. They knew.

These women had a special knowledge—a wisdom that comes only from surviving what others can't imagine. They understood discomfort—their own and others'—and still chose to see the beauty in life.

They became sources of insight and grace in my life. Though they remain in my past, I carry the memory of their strength and humility with me to this day.

Lost My Reason to Get Up Early

The cognitive impairments I live with—stemming from a hit-and-run closed head injury and compounded by aging—have left me adrift in a whirlwind of confusion: faulty memory, difficulty focusing, an inability to multitask, and a frustratingly low tolerance for stress.

Once considered by many to be the best social worker in a school district with dozens on staff, I had to walk away from the profession I spent years building. It wasn't one moment—it was a slow death stretched over several years.

I was given second chances. Opportunities to move from one school to another. The hope was that somewhere, I might find a rhythm I could manage—a space where the bureaucratic demands, caseload pressures, and administrative load of school social work wouldn't overwhelm me.

But eventually, I had to let go.

Returning to the subject of my family of origin—I think, in their estimation, I never quite grew up. I've always had long hair, a beard, worn mostly jeans and t-shirts, and kept a kind of free-spirited, offbeat innocence that's remained with me since the 1960s.

But their view of me—how they interacted with me—was shaped by more than just my appearance.

To them, I sometimes seemed immature. As an adult living with bipolar disorder, my behavior could be impulsive, reactionary, overly sensitive to criticism, and highly emotional. They may have seen my inner struggle as a failure to mature, rather than as symptoms of a condition I didn't choose.

Barry, Runner, me, Bonnie

A Lifetime Ago

How is it possible that the past existed so long ago? Most people are gone. A photo like the one above reminds me I didn't always have bipolar disorder. And like the others, my early self is gone.

Tilt-A-Whirl
I remember going to Kiddieland as a kid and riding the Tilt-A-Whirl. When I got off, I felt dizzy and queasy. A deluge of deadlines and time-sensitive obligations made me feel the same way at work. At that time, when my mind was a'swirl, I should have given time management a whirl.

The cognitive impairments I live with—stemming from a hit-and-run closed head injury, seizures, bipolar disorder, and the natural aging process—have left me adrift in a whirlwind of confusion: faulty memory, difficulty focusing, an inability to multitask, and a frustratingly low tolerance for stress.

Once considered by many to be the best social worker in a school district with dozens on staff, I had to walk away from the profession I spent years building. It wasn't a sudden ending. It was a slow death stretched over several years.

I was given second chances. Opportunities to move from one school to another. The hope was that somewhere I might find a rhythm I could manage—a setting where the bureaucratic demands, caseload pressure, and paperwork wouldn't overwhelm me.

But eventually, I had to let go. In time, even basic tasks became too much. My seizures—and the memory problems that followed—made me increasingly forgetful. I shunned paperwork, bank statements, and anything involving loans, taxes, or medical forms. I enrolled in automatic bill payment systems because I frequently lost statements or forgot to submit payments altogether.

I developed a fatalistic approach to life. I no longer existed in the world of "go-getters"—those who take the bull by the horns, bootstrap their way to success, dream big, know powerful people, and live large. That world seemed far away, even alien.

And so, I was infantilized. Well-meaning family members reminded me to take my medications and made sure I saw my general practitioner, dentist, and psychiatrist. They'd call to remind me to get more sleep, eat better, exercise. They even made contingency plans for my life after the passing of my then-94-year-old mother, who still lived nearby in Chicago and remained a steady figure in my day-to-day life.

When you live with an unaddressed mood disorder—or even a partially addressed one—major losses like this don't just trigger grief. They stir something deeper. For some, the question becomes not where to live, but whether to live.

Poem

My family always mattered
They were everything to me
I destroyed a perfect marriage
And never got it back again
My children lived with my illness
Bipolar was forced on my kids
It really wasn't fair to them

I was the youngest of three children
I was different than the rest
I was infantilized by them
As an adult I still am young
My bipolar didn't help me any
Even now they look after me
My family always mattered

Questions

If you or another family member have bipolar disorder or any mental illness, how has it affected birth family, immediate family and/or extended family life?

If the illness has contributed negatively to the family unit, what can you or family members do to minimize the problems and improve the situation?

In what ways can a parent with bipolar disorder affect the emotional and behavioral functioning of their children?
What are some possible helpful interventions?

If a child's behavior was negatively affected in school, would it be advantageous to let the administrator, social worker and your child's teachers know that the parent's bipolar disorder might be affecting their child's performance in school? Why or why not?

Guilt can be a lasting characteristic of a parent's bipolar disorder, especially when considering the effects and limitations it has placed on the family and the children. Divorce and a family breakup contributes to the devastation of bipolar disorder.
What can a family do to thrive a parent's bipolar diagnosis?

CHAPTER 9

I Hid In The
Garage Attic

Climbed Up The Ladder
Looking For An Escape
Escaping The Escape

The Way Up

It's incredible the "steps" we'll take to avoid the pain of not meeting the expectations of others and ourselves. The steps I took were on a ladder I used to inch my way up to the garage attic. It seemed enormous to me. It would have to be to take me from the cement floor all the way up to the rafters! A redwood with steps pretty much describes it. I never entertained the possibility of falling, though. I was too focused on the reality of failing.

" I spent much of my life hiding."

–Kevyn Aucoin

Bipolar pain brings me back to a place I first visited more than half a century ago. It was a hiding place—up in the attic of our family's detached, wood-framed, one-car garage
.   The only way up was our massive ten-foot wooden ladder. To me, it looked like a giant redwood with steps. Its uprights were splattered with decades of paint—like tree rings, marking the passage of time from one home project to the next.

I recognized the periwinkle pink from my older sister Bonnie's bedroom, the flat ivory from our living room, the twinkleberry blue from our bathroom, and that strange, newfangled avocado green from our kitchen—a color better suited for The Jetsons than for our modest post-WWII home.

The ladder also intimidated me. I remember holding it steady as a child while my dad climbed down after painting the ceiling. I got a nasty sliver in my palm. He had to dig it out with a needle, using the lens of an old slide projector as a makeshift magnifying glass. It was so tiny.

My dad was a bit of a Renaissance man. It was hell for me—but I suspect he thought of it as quality time with his youngest child.

Side Trip

So, what was I doing up there? And what does this have to do with the Impaired Self? Please follow me on this brief side trip—a story to further illustrate the pain of the Impaired Self.

You can try to hide the truth. You can vow to keep your bipolar disorder secret—to shield yourself from shame and your family from humiliation.

But you can't outrun it. It follows you. Creeps up from behind. Then, when you least expect it, it leaps—lands on your back, digs its claws in, and refuses to let go until it decides to.

This reminds me of a story my daughter recently shared. It was about a woman who once lived across the street from us—a kind soul and a devoted mother of two daughters. She's now in her fifties. She had bipolar disorder—long before I knew I had mine. At the time, she had it under control with medication. She lived peacefully with her husband, a soft-spoken, talented carpenter.

They eventually moved to Connecticut. But the story takes a tragic turn. She went off her meds and began using drugs heavily. She spun out of control—spiraling from mania into a depression that nearly claimed her life. She is now confined to a nursing home. Unsurprisingly, her husband divorced her. He has since started over with someone new.

She, however, is another story. While he has been building a new life, she has been slowly losing hers.

I Panicked

Now take that pain, and picture it folding into my Impaired Self—the part of me that took shape as a young boy hiding in the garage attic.

It started near report card time. I noticed an envelope from school addressed to my parents. It was thin—not the kind that included forms or information packets. So, I did what any self-respecting kid would do.

I opened it. Blood drained from my face. It was a failure notice from my basic math teacher. I panicked. My heart pounded like I was crossing the final yards of a 26-mile marathon. I imagined being yelled at by my father, humiliated once again for not being smart enough to pass basic math. He, a whiz with numbers and business. Me, the dumb one.

So, I escaped. To nowhere. The way to nowhere was straight up that old wooden ladder, into the attic. A place no one would willingly inhabit. No one would visit it for any reason. The perfect place to just… disappear.

That's how my Impaired Self saw me. I wasn't a boy. I wasn't even a person. I was something closer to dirt and spider webs. Skin, organs, tissue—all tucked into a dark, nasty corner where no self-respecting soul would dare to be. I wasn't part of the house below me—a house full of people who could hold jobs, succeed in school, and, most baffling of all, be happy.

Eye Contact

I left a note saying I was running away—and that I'd return someday. I heard voices searching for me in the garage, just below where I was hiding.

From my attic perch, I felt like a Greek god among the clouds, listening to the lowly humans below pondering life's great mysteries, such as:

"Where is David?

Hiding My Fear

The garage attic was always a mystery to me. It was too high to peer into from ground level and too high to risk a tumble from a ladder. All that went by the wayside when a class failure notice was involved. Imagine how such a message can motivate kids to risk their safety to protect themselves from harsh judgment. The only thing worse than falling is failing.

Eye to Eye

The saying "seeing eye to eye" means something different than the context of this image when being harshly chastised by a "loving" parent. Far from being in agreement, there is extreme dissonance. It's safe to say the looks in this image appear to be "polar" opposites, perhaps a foreshadowing of acquiring bipolar disorder decades down the road.

Eventually, I had to go to the bathroom—and just enough self-respect remained to stop me from going in my pants. So I made the rickety descent down from Mount Olympus to the garage's cement floor, rushed to the back door, and slipped into the house as if nothing unusual had happened.

I glanced at myself in the bathroom mirror. I was completely covered in dirt and grime—ready to blend in with any dumpster or garbage heap, like I was taking cover during a national invasion. But the only aggressor I encountered was my father.

For the life of me, I can't recall what happened when our eyes met.
And to be honest, I'm not trying to dig it up. I've chosen to let that sleeping dog lie. I know it was bad. And more importantly, the salient part of this story has already been told.

External Causation

I share this incident not to blame, but to illuminate. This story brings attention to the Impaired Self—not just in me, but in many of us who live with mental illness, cognitive challenges, or other disabilities.

Just as my father, likely without meaning to, contributed to the development of my Impaired Self, so too can the most caring and loving family members and friends inadvertently reinforce it in others.

We all hide in our own ways. My friend hid behind suicide. My neighbor behind drugs. And me? I hid in a garage attic.

What about you—or someone you know? Do you hide behind gambling? Smoking? Alcohol or drug dependence? Compulsive spending or overachievement?

It makes me wonder: Where are our hurting children hiding? Behind cutting? Bullying? Self-victimization?

These behaviors are too often labeled as "problems"—symptoms of weak adults or troubled children. But I see them as effects of a stigmatizing society—a society that instills shame, robs identity, and perpetuates the Impaired Self in those who are already vulnerable.

If parents, guardians, teachers, doctors, and service providers are to be part of the solution—not the problem—they must understand and respond with clarity and compassion. To help our children develop dignity, self-respect, and joy in life, they must first understand:

- How the Impaired Self forms in our children

- How society creates and perpetuates it

- How we can help them develop an Integrated Self

Poem

I hid in the garage attic

I was escaping to nowhere

I tried to lose myself up there

No one else found me, but I did

My impairments followed me there

I tried to escape from stigma

And I still do so to this day

A place where no one wants to be

A dark corner and stigmatized

To rid it, you must integrate

Accept all of your impairments

Find and embrace your many strengths

And then find yourself at great lengths

I hid in the garage attic

Questions

Major mental illness can impact the integrity of a marriage or close relationship, often leaving them in tatters. Is it possible for a marriage or close relationship to survive when the emotional survival of the individual is tenuous? If so, what might help the marriage or close relationship survive? How could someone's mental illness obstruct those attempts?

Running away from problems can put some distance between feeling defeat, pain, and failure. Sooner or later, one has to return, only to find the problem still exists. Have you run from a problem, either literally or figuratively? What did it accomplish? Was it counterproductive? If so, how?

Do your friends or family members inadvertently contribute to your Impaired Self? If so, how? What possible interventions can you put into place to mitigate their negative influence?

CHAPTER 10

We Can Repair
The Impairment

The Integrated Self
Helping Ourselves
Defying Stigma

A New Day. An Old Way.

With bipolar disorder, it's very easy for every day to feel the same, whether you are feeling even, depressed, or manic. Why? Because of the stigma that underlies it all. And the awareness that you are different. That's the part that feels the same every day. I'm feeling balanced and healthy? Oh yeah, I'm bipolar. I'm feeling depressed? Oh yeah, I'm bipolar. I'm feeling manic? Oh yeah, I'm bipolar. And then there is the moment when you forget you are bipolar, and the sun comes out and the clouds disperse. And then, for a brief moment… the negative effects of stigma are gone.

"The first step towards getting somewhere is to decide you're not going to stay where you are."

–J.P. Morgan

I have presented my bipolar narrative and introduced the concept of the Impaired Self, along with its negative characteristics and effects. What remains is to describe the path I have personally taken—from the "cracked window" of the Impaired Self to the "clear window" of the Integrated Self:

- Commit to learning about bipolar disorder

- Acknowledge and accept that you have the illness

- Recognize stigma and understand how it affects you

These foundational steps are essential. They represent and ultimately determine the extent to which a person living with bipolar disorder and its stigma can achieve a high-quality life (Mancini & Rogers, 2007).

Online and On Time

In addition to receiving therapy and taking prescribed medication, you can become your own best advocate by seeking out educational and self-help resources online. Use search terms such as bipolar stigma, bipolar coping, bipolar support, bipolar support groups, bipolar self-help, bipolar medical management, and bipolar crisis intervention.

Resources like those found in the References and Resources section of this book can be powerful tools. The more knowledge and insight you gain, the more equipped you are to manage your illness and reclaim control of your life.

Social Support

One intervention I've found invaluable is attending clinician-led support groups in outpatient hospital settings. These groups combine psychotherapy and education within a strengths-based, affirming environment.

Support naturally grows within the group while therapeutic strategies—such as problem-solving, role-playing, stress management, and coping skills—are introduced and practiced. These groups also offer the chance to better understand your illness through the lens of personal experience, as it relates to your relationships, environments, and life situations.

Acceptance

With a clear grasp of the Bipolar Impaired Self—a concept that first emerged from students' reflections on my artwork at Serendip and has guided every piece I have made since—I have learned to convert the raw negatives of bipolar disorder and stigma into a balanced, confident sense of identity.

Accepting our diagnosis can open entire worlds. Research links bipolar disorder to heightened creativity, and we can steer that gift more reliably when we sustain a healthy lifestyle: nourishing food, consistent sleep, stress-management practices, medication adherence, and early action to head off swings into depression or mania.

Perhaps most crucial is our skill at deflecting stigma. We know how judgment can pierce the heart like a poisoned arrow. Today, those arrows glance off, barely scratching the surface of a once-vulnerable Impaired Self.

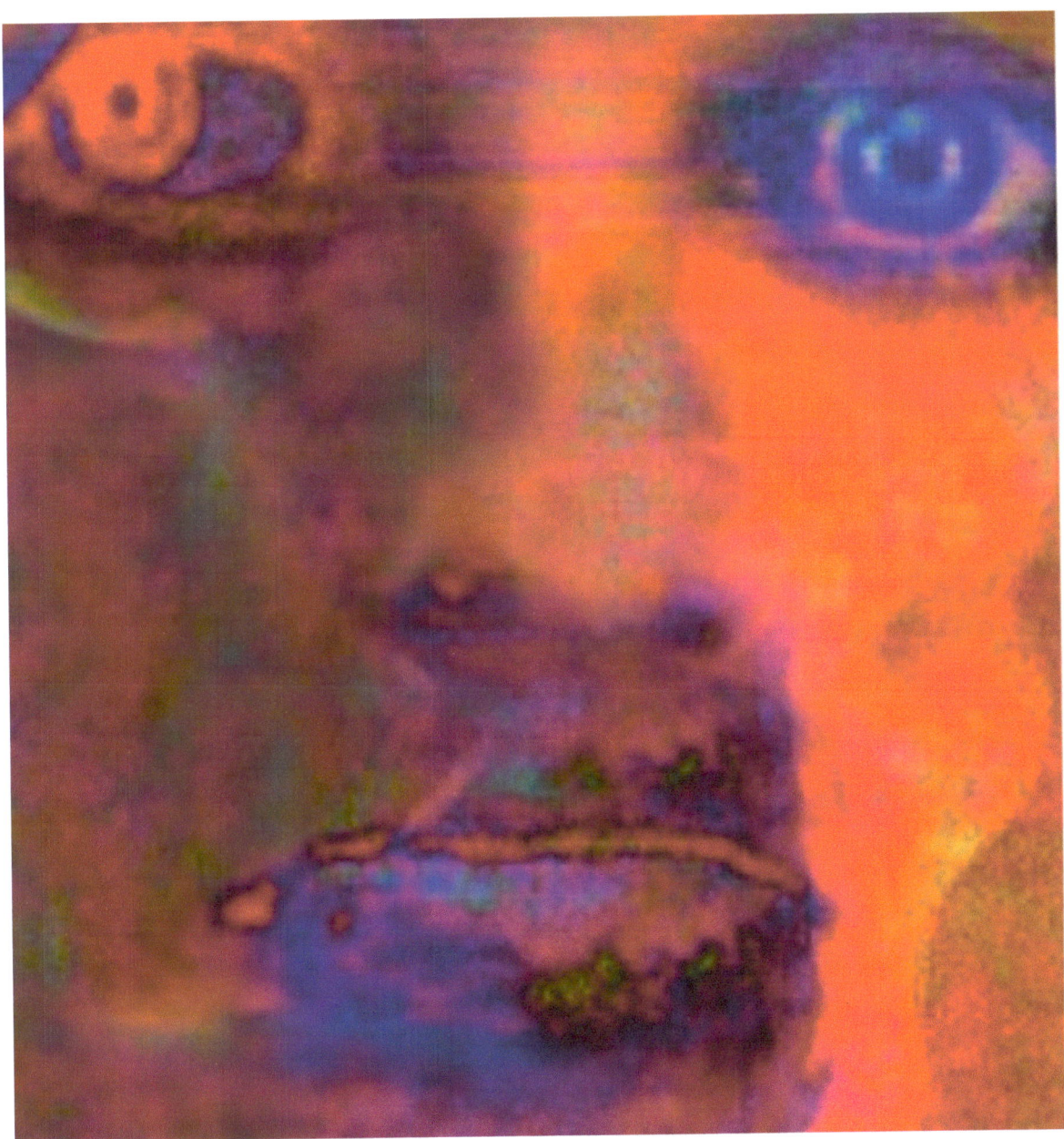

Caught Off-Guard

When I recognized the concept of the Bipolar Impaired Self and its relation to stigma and the self, I was stunned. It caught me off guard. They call it an "aha!" experience. Mine was more "Eureka." It wasn't the glitter of gold I discovered but the crystal-clear window of the integrated bipolar self.

Poem

We can repair the impairment

We can all clear our cracked windows

We don't need stigma to rule us

We can lead ourselves to freedom

We must know about bipolar

We can be bipolar and proud

We can then accept who we are

We can love all of who we are

We can eliminate stigma

We can see a better future

We can eliminate all shame

We can do without regret

We can work to make it happen

We can repair the impairment

Questions

Making oneself more knowledgeable about one's affliction contributes to understanding and self-acceptance. Seeking to become more knowledgeable is not an automatic response by people with mental illness. Why do you think individuals may not seek help for their diagnosis-related challenges?

Social support in a therapeutic group setting can be a helpful and positive intervention. What would you say is the difference between social support in a therapeutic group setting versus social support in the natural environment? Can both be equally effective?
Why or why not?

Has there been a time in your life when psychiatric symptoms of stigma ill-effects required more integration between your self and your Impaired Self? Did you apply any interventions to help integrate? What worked? What didn't? Why or why not?

CHAPTER 11

Know The
Iceberg Model

Tip Of The Iceberg
Beneath The Iceberg
Interventions

Recognizing the Iceberg
There are two parts to the Iceberg Model. It consists of the top portion of the iceberg—medication and psychotherapy for managing bipolar symptoms, as well as the bottom portion of the iceberg—therapy, education, and self-help for understanding and coping with bipolar stigma.

"To know what you know and what you do not know, that is true knowledge."

—Confucius

Throughout this book, we've seen how stigma and the sense of self are often absent from general discussions of bipolar disorder—even in psychotherapeutic settings. But when we integrate these often-overlooked aspects with traditional symptom management, we create a more powerful, more human model of treatment: one that recognizes the whole person.

Dealing with bipolar stigma begins with knowing oneself. That means looking below the tip of the iceberg—into the connections between stigma, the self, the Impaired Self, and the bipolar disorder itself. With this deeper awareness, life can become not just manageable, but meaningful.

The Iceberg Model encourages therapists and clients—and those on a self-help path—to explore what often remains hidden: the emotional and psychological consequences of stigma. Too often, people with a bipolar diagnosis are left uninformed about how stigma quietly undermines their functioning, their identity, and their confidence. The Iceberg Model brings those truths to the surface, helping to integrate the stigma-infused Impaired Self into a fuller, more balanced understanding of who we are.

The symptoms of bipolar disorder, combined with the wounds of stigma, can shatter one's self-image and sense of stability. From the outside, we may appear odd, unpredictable—even dangerous. But inside, we are innocent victims of an illness we did not cause, did not deserve, and never asked for.

While we fight to stay afloat against the gale-force winds of mental illness—on battlefields others never see—all we ask is this:

Put aside your prejudices. Open your minds enough to truly know us, and your hearts enough to truly accept us.

Bipolar/Bipolar Stigma Symptoms

Bipolar Symptoms

- Mania

- Depression

- Risky Behavior

- Spending Sprees

- Mood Swings

- Hypersexuality

- Rapid Cycling

- Irritability

- Self Harm

- Suicidal Ideation

Bipolar Stigma Symptoms

- Lethargy

- Anxiety

- Insecurity

- Inadequacy

- Inferiority

- Hopelessness

- Pessimism

- Fear

- Confusion

- Self-Harm

- Isolation

- Health Deterioration

- Suicidal Ideation

Interventions

**Bipolar Disorder
Interventions
*(Top of the Iceberg)***
Medication
Psychotherapy
Self-Help

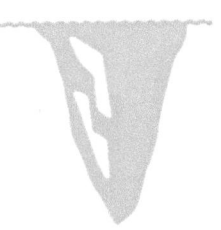

**Bipolar Stigma
Interventions
*(Bottom of the Iceberg)***
Stigma Awareness
Self-Help

**Bipolar Disorder and
Bipolar Stigma Interventions
*(Top AND Bottom of the Iceberg)***
Medication
Psychotherapy
Stigma Awareness
Self-Help

Tools

Use the Following 3-Part Tool Kit On Your Own Or With Your Therapist to:

- Become aware of bipolar stigma issues

- Recognize the pitfalls of bipolar stigma

- Recognize if you are affected by bipolar stigma

- Help avert bipolar stigma problems

- Assist in gathering bipolar stigma information

"I would like to talk about my bipolar identity today."

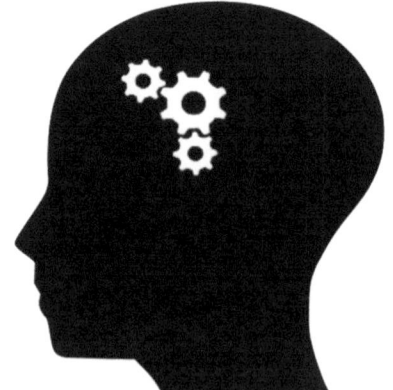

"Very good. Let's begin."

Part 1

The Following Are Common Bipolar Stigma Symptoms You Should Be Aware Of And Share With Your Therapist, As Needed.

- Agitation

- Lethargy

- Fear

- Pessimism

- Confusion

- Inferiority

- Helplessness

- Hopelessness

- Neediness

- Inadequacy

- Low Self-Esteem

- Decreased Self-Care

- Suicidality

Part 2

The Following Issues Can Occur From Bipolar Stigmatization. Become Aware Of Them And Discuss With Your Therapist, as Needed.

- Employment Restrictions

- Child Custody Restrictions

- Feeling Shame

- Being Shunned

- Being Stereotyped

- Being Socially Excluded

- Being Labeled

- Being Infantilized

- Being Intellectually Minimized

- Being Brunt of Jokes

- Controlling Who Knows You Have
  Bipolar Disorder

- Social Self-Consciousness

Part 3

Consider The Following Interventions To Help You Cope With Your Bipolar Diagnosis And Bipolar Stigma.

- Accept your bipolar diagnosis
- Recognize your successes
- Accept your shortcomings
- Be aware you are more than your diagnosis
- Be assertive and communicate your needs
- Go for therapy
- Take your meds as prescribed
- Be invested in your therapy
- Play an active role in therapy
- Seek out articles and books about bipolar stigma
- Lead a healthy lifestyle
- Cut yourself some slack
- Pursue personal interests: take an art class; listen to music; learn and play a musical instrument; read/write; take a class; go for walks; connect with family and friends; meditate; join a Meetup group or create your own; put together a photo album or scrapbook; engage in fun sports or exercise activities; rediscover your ethnic, cultural, and religious roots and family tree; volunteer
- Remember that you, like all people are unique, and worthy of respect

Poem

Know the iceberg model
We did not know that it was stigma
We sensed it was always there
We should consider the iceberg
There is the top of the iceberg
And then there is the bottom
We can repair the impairment

Top is the behavior we see
Bottom is the stigma we don't
We call knowing both true wisdom
We need to think about it
We need to work with it
And we need to integrate it
Know the iceberg model

Questions

Stigma is largely absent from most bipolar discussions and treatment recommendations. Why do you think that is?

How can discussing stigma aid in therapy for mental illness?

Do you think an iceberg model for treating bipolar disorder is more effective than using the traditional single model? Why or why not?

Would a therapist resist using the iceberg model in their therapy sessions? Why or why not?"

CHAPTER 12

We Understand The Impaired Self

School Classroom
Doctor's Office
Psych Ward

Letting Go

Going forward, making progress, and advancing our reach all require letting go. Let go of doubts, let go of fears, let go of hesitation, and let go of our stranglehold on pessimism. It takes the inquisitiveness and curiosity of a child to get us there. It takes the wisdom of someone experienced, mature, and familiar with overcoming struggle to keep us on a path toward further growth and development, as a person and as a society.

"We cannot solve our problems with the same thinking we used when we created them."

–Albert Einstein

I would like to share three personal vignettes that further reinforce the need for understanding and applying the concept of the Impaired Self to individuals with impairments and disabilities. I draw upon my own experiences through the telling of stories to bring an immediacy and sense of reality to the situation.

As noted in my preface, what better way for us to be an authority on a given topic than to be the subject of experience and author of its description? I, as well as others have been directly affected and influenced by those in positions of power and control.

These are instances where the dignity and self-respect of the individual, especially those with disabilities, can be acknowledged and nurtured, as opposed to neglected or overlooked.

Education

As a school social worker, my professional focus was students' social and emotional development. But what about my lived experience with bipolar disorder? What about the concepts explored in this book? How might they take root and grow within the educational system—changing how we help students not just cope, but thrive?

Students shouldn't be seen as just a set of behaviors to eliminate or reinforce. They are human beings with emotional lives that often go unnoticed. Some come to school carrying problems so big, so heavy, that they eclipse everything else: homework, social rules, or even the ability to ask for help with a math assignment.

What if we began recognizing the Impaired Self in children with disabilities—not just their learning needs, but the quiet injuries to their self-image and sense of worth caused by stigma? That understanding might shift the way we relate to them—and the way we teach them.

Maybe it would help a teacher show more patience to a student with an anxiety disorder who's too afraid to enter the classroom.

Maybe it would reframe the judgment of a child who overreacts when asked to let someone cut in line.

And maybe—just maybe—it would reduce the venting in staff rooms and increase the empathy in classrooms.

If we can begin to see the stigmatized self behind the disability, we can begin to heal—not just teach.

"Did You Write This???"

As a student, all I wanted was recognition—not just for trying, but for being me. I'll never forget what happened in grade school. I was struggling in most of my classes due to undiagnosed learning differences and had no idea I might have a talent for writing. I was too focused on grammar, punctuation, and doing things "right" to see any creative potential in myself.

One day, we were assigned a paper on a book we had read. I don't remember the book, but I do remember how deeply it moved me. I dove into its meaning and symbolism, letting loose with everything I felt. For the first time, I ignored the mechanics and gave myself permission to simply express. For a moment, I didn't feel impaired—I felt free.

When the paper came back, that feeling vanished. At the top of the page, in red ink, was a large circled "F," and next to it, the question: "Did you write this????"

I didn't just fall—I nosedived.

According to my teacher, someone like me—with poor grades and a scattered academic record—couldn't have possibly written something so insightful. I was devastated. I had been seen, but only to be doubted.

Years later, while writing my doctoral dissertation, I realized that this moment was one of the earliest wounds to my emerging sense of self. That teacher's disbelief didn't just challenge my writing—it cracked the window through which I saw my own worth.

Psychiatric Hospitalizations

It was my second psychiatric hospitalization.

I was wheeled into the emergency room with all the dignity of a damaged UPS package—taped together, barcoded, and shuttled off without ceremony.

We passed row after row of curtained bays where patients were being cared for, spoken to, touched. I, however, was wheeled into a locked, guarded room just large enough for a single bed. No window. No chair. No human presence.

I lay there alone for six hours. No food. No water. No explanation. Just a door that stayed closed.

Eventually, someone I never saw before—and would never see again—came to tell me that I was being transferred to another hospital, about thirty minutes away, for "treatment."

No discussion. No acknowledgment. Just one more trip in a long chain of institutional indifference.

Student's Passing Mark or Teacher's Remark in Passing?
Students have to work to succeed in school, as reflected by earning good grades. How many teachers could "make the grade" in relating to students in such a way as to help prevent or eliminate their Impaired Selves?

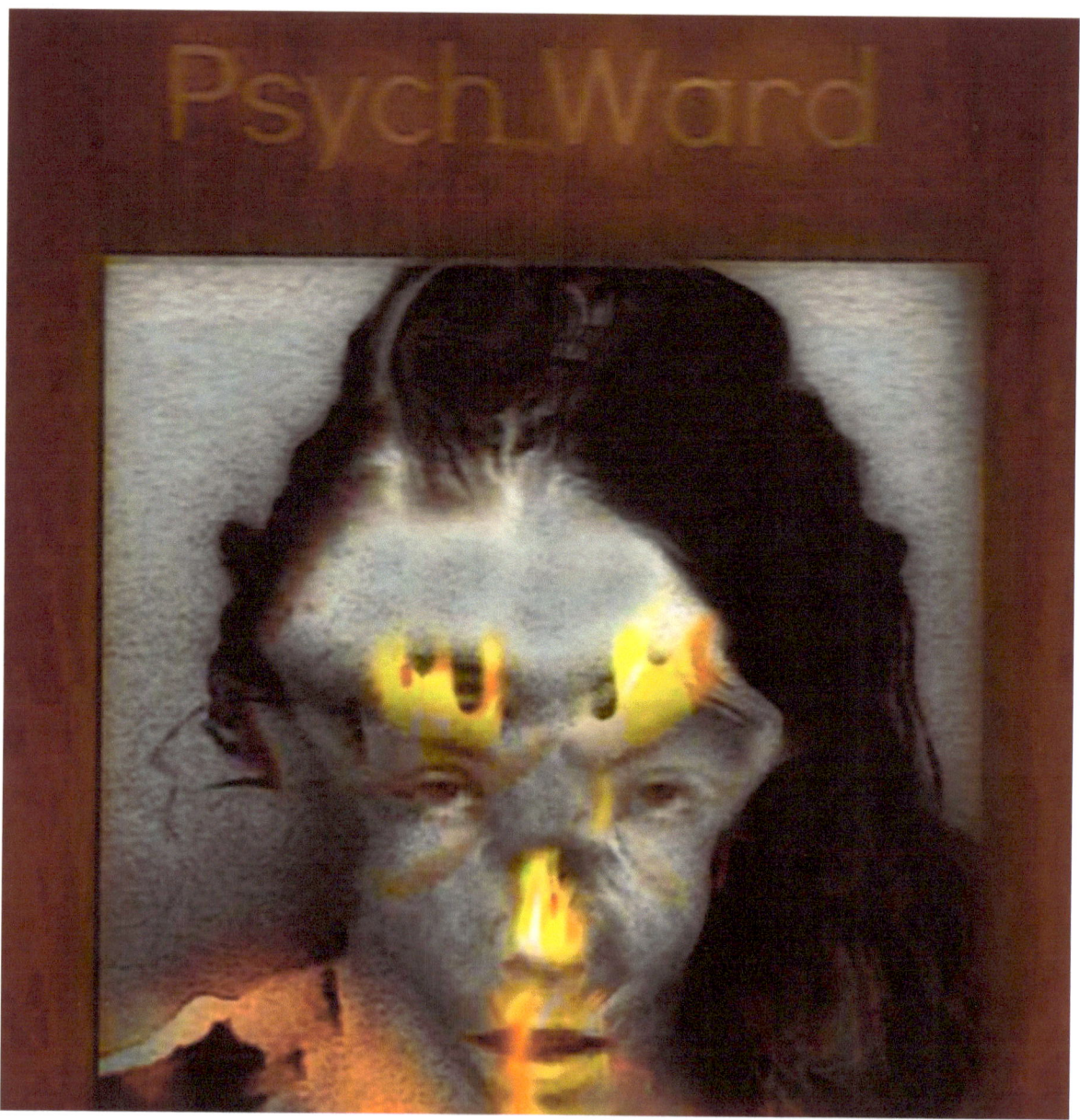

Psycho

Thank you, Alfred Hitchcock, for that enduring vision of mental illness: Norman Bates, "Psycho's" deranged, misanthropic killer. In Ken Kesey's "One Flew Over the Cuckoo's Nest," we are also presented with a group of social misfits portrayed by people with mental illness. No wonder real people with mental illness get burned by the media while their reputations go up in smoke.

Psych Ward

What does that kind of detached, bureaucratic attention do to someone in the midst of a psychiatric crisis?

It doesn't take a Sigmund Freud to guess that it's not in their best interest. A little empathic concern or a few words of explanation could have made all the difference. Instead, I waited a total of nine hours with no real human connection—just an afterthought meal, delivered cold, with a barely silent indifference.

When someone finally arrived, they didn't offer care or insight—just a few perfunctory questions, as if checking a box.

My empty food tray sat there, untouched, like a forgotten patient waiting for a bedpan.

In the throes of a bipolar depressive or manic episode, experiences like this don't just hurt—they shape you. They affirm the belief that you're not worth responding to. Not worth seeing.

A Prescription for Physician Understanding

In the past, I avoided going to my general practitioner. Not because she was aloof—quite the opposite. She's warm, attentive, and one of those rare physicians who doesn't double-book or rush you out the door in under seven minutes. I've seen doctors who could really benefit from wearing rollerblades. Not her.

And yet, there were times I wished she would hurry me out. Instead, I sat there feeling like a ten-year-old under gentle but unmistakable reprimand. Her brows would knit together in quiet disapproval as she reviewed my labs.

I needed to lose thirty pounds, adjust my diet to lower my cholesterol and blood pressure, and exercise regularly. Instead, I got her version of the "Do you want to live or die?" lecture. Subtle, but brutal.

I'd leave her office feeling chastened, tail tucked, hoping to emotionally recover on the ride home. But even that wasn't easy. As my tires crunched over the gravel in her driveway, I imagined the stones whispering, *don't get any more kidney stones*. I had lost the last one I passed—supposed to save it for lab testing. We were both mildly heartbroken about it.

So where does the Impaired Self fit into all this? I believe there's a fundamental disconnect between physician care and physician caring. Like schools and psych units, the doctor's office often becomes a place where symptoms are cataloged, behaviors are judged, and prescriptions are written—all with little room for the messy emotional terrain that comes with being human, especially one with a disability.

As someone living with an Impaired Self, the moment my doctor starts outlining a health plan, I'm not just hearing about lifestyle changes—I'm absorbing it through the distorted filter of internalized flaws and failures. Her expectations are clear. But the distance between her medical logic and my emotional reality can feel vast.

Maybe what looks like laziness, denial, or noncompliance is actually something quieter and more insidious—a conflict between my conscious desire to change and the whispering voice of the Impaired Self, reminding me that I've failed before.

The Impaired Self is not an excuse. It's an entry point. If physicians could recognize this—not pathologize it, but understand it—then treatment could become a partnership, not a prescription. The doctor-patient relationship could transform from one of critique and compliance to one of empathy, mutual respect, and realistic progress.

In that light, maybe following doctor's orders wouldn't feel like such a bitter pill to swallow.

To Cause No Harm

The trust we put in doctors and their Hippocratic oaths is sacred. However, we usually place physician/patient relationships and bedside manners as optional and 'frosting on the cake.' Instead, they should be given priority. If not, getting medical treatment can be a real pill.

Poem

We understand the Impaired Self
People in power must know, too
For our dignity and respect
They must see their knowledge through
It happens in all of our schools
Teachers can't miss a chance to raise
Self-esteem with every praise

Places where I'd rather be
Psych wards take our dignity
To give it back would set us free
Doctors' efforts make us well
There's always things they could say
To integrate and make our day
We understand the Impaired Self

Questions

Why do you think teachers do not automatically consider a student's Impaired Self?

Describe a situation involving you or someone you observed when a teacher contributed to the Impaired Self. How did you or the student react?

Recall a situation in the psych ward in Chapter 7 that contributed to the Impaired Self. How did it contribute? How could it have been prevented?

Do you believe your doctor(s) would be open to incorporating the Impaired Self-concept with patients in their practice? Why or why not?

CHAPTER 13

You Can Make My Burden Lighter

Impaired Self
Social Change
Determination And Dedication

Looking to the Future

It's entirely possible to have bipolar disorder and still see the positive in life and dreams in your future. It takes dedication to achieve and maintain good mental and physical health, flexibility to roll with the punches, and determination to do it all over again… and again… and again… and again.

"In order to carry a positive action we must develop here a positive vision."

–Dalai Lama

For the first time, I could picture a future in which my art cleared a path—not just for survival, but for genuine thriving within the bipolar experience.

And I'm happy to report that clarity arrived: I saw with my own eyes, and through the sparkling window of a newly integrated self, I reached a point where I could finally look beyond past doubts, failures, and disappointments.

I could begin to envision a future—one in which my art carved a path forward, helping me not just to survive, but to thrive within the bipolar experience.

And I'm happy to say that I did begin to see clearly—not only through my own eyes, but through the sparkling window of a newly integrated self.

Epiphany

Sudden insights lift the veil of denial and resistance that clouds our understanding of mental illness—both our own and others'. This book's purpose is to bring bipolar disorder, and the people who live with it, into sharper focus.

I call upon society to offer a humanistic, compassionate acceptance. May the art in these pages—which carried me through my darkest hours—also guide you toward greater understanding and fuel your resolve to end the scourge of bipolar stigma.

Poem

You can make my burden lighter
Know you contribute to my mood
Take a moment to understand
Some of the things you say and do
Please try to think before you speak
Social policies can be made
You can give my disorder honor

And do remember artwork's role
It saved my body, mind, and soul
You could be a "freedom fighter"
In truth, sickness lies not in me
It lies within society
You can make my self grow brighter
You can make my burden lighter

Questions

What are some things in your life where positives and negatives combine in a harmonious way?

Do you see the Impaired Self as a universal concept wherein all people have the potential to experience it? If so, in what ways can a universal understanding of the Impaired Self help individuals and society?

How do you think society can eliminate mental illness stigma? What roles do mainstream and social media play in the perpetuation of an end to stigma?

"Eye of the Beholder"

Afterword
Two Defects Of Perception

I am fortunate to have a significant other who cares about me and sees me as a person through unobstructed eyes. She is unfazed by bipolar stigma and its negative reputation to those of us with a bipolar diagnosis. She is a retired nurse and has seen much suffering in her many years of service, but she feels it is a travesty that society contributes to the needless suffering of individuals with bipolar stigma.

She sees me clearly, much like a healthy eye sees the world without distortion. An aberration in the eye's lens distorts and blurs the true quality of the object before it. It is called an astigmatism. It is a defect in the cornea or lens that interferes with clear and accurate vision.

The same is true for bipolar stigma. It is the astigmatism of perception that someone has for an individual with bipolar disorder. It is a defect of judgment, which blurs and distorts the positive nature of the person being judged.

In medicine, astigmatism of the eyes is treated with corrective lenses, leading to a clearer and more accurate view of objects. In this book, astigmatism of bipolar judgment has been treated with corrective words and visceral art images, leading to a more clear and accurate view of people with bipolar disorder.

After years of accepting and perpetuating mental illness stigma, we can finally turn things around and "nurse" ourselves and others to a greater sense of value and worth.

Carry on!

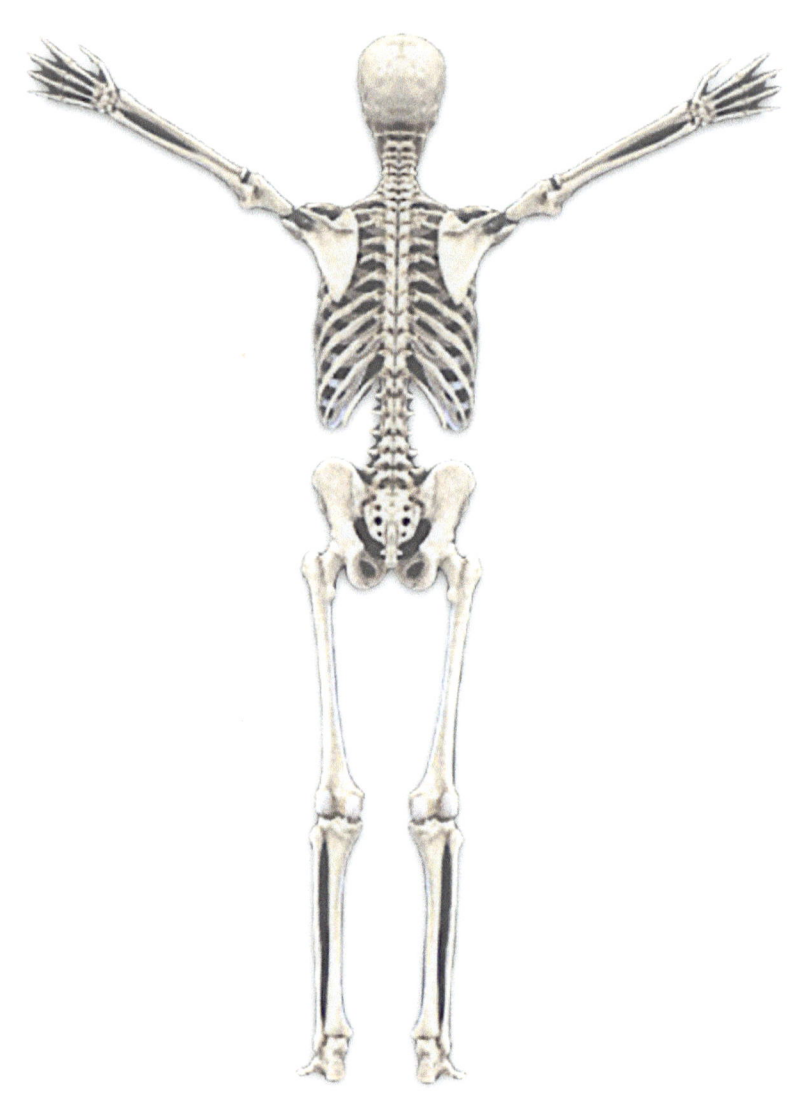

Back Matter

A Leg Up

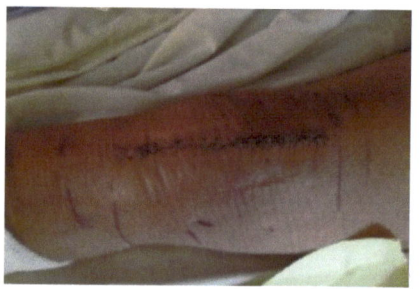

I never remember not doing artwork. I recall drawing simple portraits on paper plates that my mother gave me specifically for that purpose.

My compositions were centered on the plates, which then provided a ready-made frame for my "masterpiece." A short-lived gallery would grace our kitchen walls from time to time, providing me with exclusive one-person exhibits.

I have since graduated from crayons to a MacBook Pro computer. When I first started making my bipolar images, I had no real preconception how I would put them together. All I knew was that I had an overwhelming urge to make pictures.

I distinctly remember sitting at my computer, grabbing pictures from my phone and the Internet, melding them with surgical precision, and "working into them" with various photo enhancement applications.

As I continued along, I learned the programs and developed techniques that reflected my own visual vocabulary and aesthetic. These two images present an excellent example of how my artwork develops. The photo above is of my sister-in-law's leg after receiving her knee replacement surgery. She sent me the picture and said, "Do something with it."

The image to the right is my visual interpretation: "The Mystery of Knee Replacement Surgery." Notice how the staples become the mouth.

"The Mystery of Knee Replacement Surgery"

A Crazy Connection

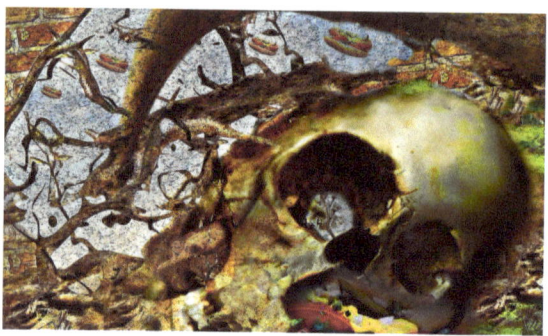

A long-standing controversy exists concerning the link between mental illness, creativity, and art—three elements that run throughout this text.

One end of the continuum believes there is no connection by rejecting the centuries-old romantic view of the "tortured artist."

On the other end of the continuum lies the belief that there is such a connection based on examples of famous artists who meet clinical diagnostic criteria for mental illness along with creativity, artistic skills, and intuitive insight. In addition, there is scientific inquiry, which supports the connection between mental illness, creativity, and art. I identify with this group.

Those Who Deny the Connection

Those who deny the link between mental illness, creativity, and art are concerned that individuals who need therapy and medication will go without help due to their pursuit of maximum artistic creativity, which is "mistakenly" associated with having a mental illness.

There is also the argument that not all great artists have a mental illness. Also taken into account are the minions of everyday creative people from all walks of life without a mental illness.

Those Who Support the Connection

A 1.2 million-person Swedish study by researchers at the Karolinska Institutet paints a different picture. The research showed artists are more prone to having schizophrenia, bipolar disorder, schizoaffective disorder, depression, anxiety disorder, alcohol abuse, drug abuse, autism, ADHD, and suicide compared to the general population.

The key to understanding the connection between mental illness, creativity, and art is what neuroscience researchers discovered to be a link between creativity and schizotypy, as well as bipolar disorder.

The inability to suppress the unnecessary cognitive activity associated with these psychological disorders, consisting of stimuli and events paired with overlapping mental processes, leads to more creative thinking.

A deluge of random, even generally mundane information, combined with heightened insight and blended with unique associations, is found to be the basis of psychopathology and high creative achievement.

Finally, from a psychodynamic self-help perspective, there is a close connection between creativity, art, and mental illness. As researcher Shelly Carson, Ph.D., states, "Creative work acts as a kind of self-administered therapy."

Emotional Connections

My art fits within the Expressionism movement, which originated in Germany at the beginning of the 20th century.

Expressionist artists focus on expressing emotions instead of images based on objective reality, such as landscapes, still lives, the human figure, etc.

Expressionist artists such as Vincent van Gogh, Edvard Munch, Francisco Goya, and Francis Bacon display dark emotional undertones in their work, depicting fear, distress, and more intense and ghastly, macabre imagery.

You will recall early in this book that Aristotle refers to art as representing the inner significance of things as opposed to their outward appearances. This definitely describes Expressionist artwork and is a very impressive comment by Aristitotle, considering he lived between 384 and 322 BCE! Notice how each of these art pieces elicit feeling emanating from the expressive work of the artist.

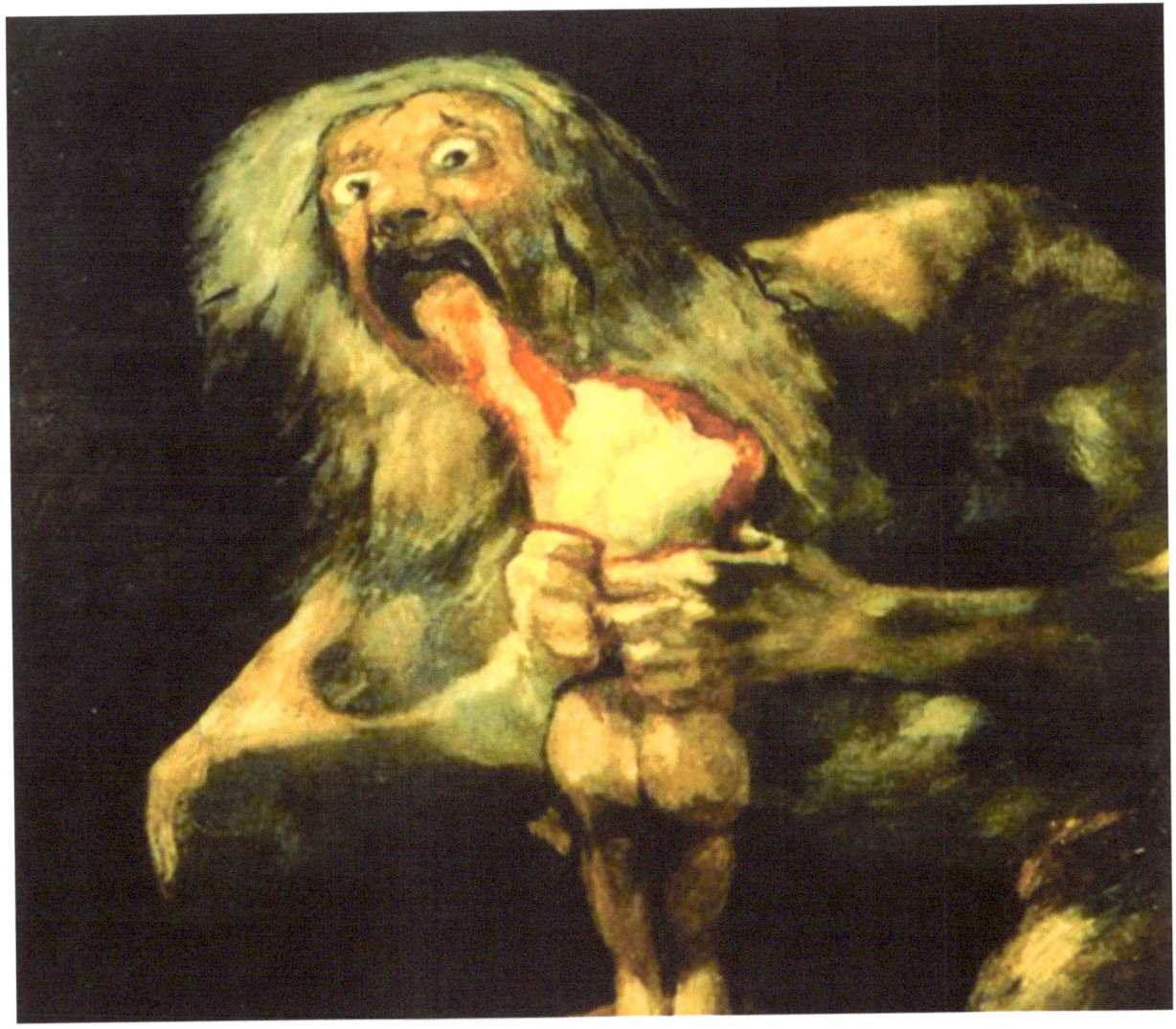

Left:
Francis Bacon *Diagnosis: Depression*
"Screaming Pope" 1949

Above:
Francisco Goya *Diagnosis: Depression*
"Saturn Devouring His Son" 1820-1823

More From Within

A Selection From 400 Images

Every square that follows is a window into my lived experience with bipolar disorder.
Together they chart the distance between stigma and self-acceptance—one honest image at a time.

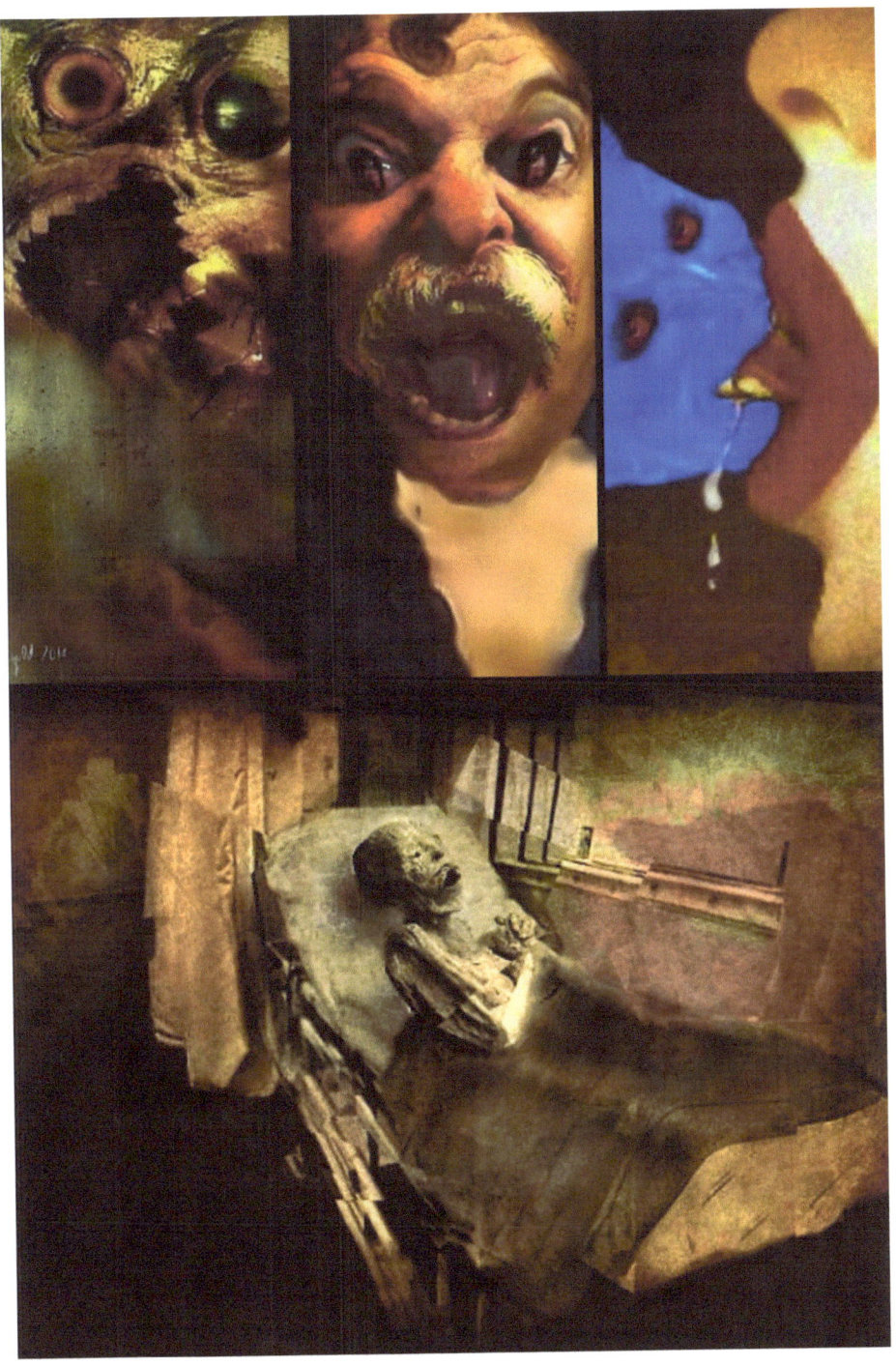

David A. Feingold, Ed.D

Biography

David Feingold was born in Chicago, Illinois. He works in the medium of digital art to present the inner struggles of those with psychiatric diagnoses. His art brings awareness of the stigma and prejudice associated with all mental illnesses. Feingold has a broad education and professional background, which, along with his personal experience with bipolar disorder, influence much of his Art: a Bachelor's in Art Education, a Master's in Visual Design, a Master's in Social Work, and a Doctorate in Disability Studies.

His work is represented in numerous venues, including National Public Radio, museums and art centers, professional journals, poetry and music collaborations, and inclusions in the permanent art collection of the Universal Design Accessible Living Laboratory for architectural advancement; The Ryan Licht Sang Bipolar Foundation; and the Stiles-Nicholson Brain Institute.

Feingold worked for 15 years as a visual designer and 15 years as a clinical social worker. He had to take early retirement due to advancing cognitive impairments stemming from an auto hit-and-run closed head injury. The head injury was also the genesis of his seizure and bipolar disorders.

He recently moved from his vibrant Lakeview neighborhood in Chicago, just blocks away from Wrigley Field, to be closer to his vibrant significant other in the northern suburbs. He says, however, he can still hear the Chicago Cubs' crack of the bat in his quiet moments.

The Road Ahead

This book has been a long time in the making--
not just in years, but in the path it took
to arrive in your hands.

It was shaped by silence and doubt, and by
a quiet insistence that stories like mine
could offer something to others--something
real, something shared, something that
pushes back against stigma with truth.

If these pages reflected even part of your
own experience, or helped you see someone
you love more clearly, then the effort was
worth it.

Thank you for walking this path with me.
May it stay with you, and may you pass it on.

- David A. Feingold

Resources

Alberta Health Services

Mental health awareness resources for schools.
Elementary school student mental health awareness kit.
https://www.albertahealthservices.ca/info/Page13368.aspx

Junior high school student mental health awareness kit

https://www.albertahealthservices.ca/info/Page13367.aspx

Bipolar Disorder in Children/Smarter Parenting

Offers healthy guide, parent tips and information in support of parenting children with bipolar disorder
https://www.smarterparenting.com/behavioral-issues/ bipolar/

Children's Health

How parents can help their child understand mental health stigma.
https://www.childrens.com/health-wellness/5-ways-to-end-mental-health-stigma

College Campus Stigma Reduction Activities

Extensive resource for stigma awareness and reduction activities for college students. https://www.cccstudentmentalhealth.org/docs/CCC-Stigma-Reduction-Fact-Sheet.pdf *Alberta Health Services*

Resources

DBSA Depression and Bipolar Support

Offers support, services, and resources with local support groups, audio and video casts, and printed materials. https://www.dbsalliance.org/

Learning for Justice

"Demystifying the Mind Toolkit" Introduces ways to provide mental health literacy in schools. https://www.learningforjustice.org/magazine/spring-2019/demystifying-the-mind

Make It OK.org

Tools and opportunities to teach, share, learn, and speak about mental illnesses and stigma; read other people's stories and submit your own about mental illness stigma.

NAMI/National Alliance on Mental Illness

In-person and online mental health awareness presentations to students and youth groups. https://www.nami.org/Support-Education/Mental-Health-Education/NAMI-Ending-the-Silence

PBS "Erasing the Stigma" Video

Explores and discusses mental illness stigma in the media and society. https://www.ket.org/program/health-three60/erasing-the-stigma-of-mental-illness-30765/

Resources

Ryan Licht Sang Bipolar Foundation

An initiative dedicated to erasing stigma associated with bipolar disorder and funding research to develop an empirical test to screen for early detection of bipolar disorder in children.
https://www.ryanlichtsangbipolarfoundation.org/

Sinclair P. Ceaser III, Mental Health Speaker

Helps people unlearn shame around mental illness.
https://sinclairceasar.com

TED Talks

Many excellent video presentations on mental health and stigma awareness https://www.ted.com/search?q=stigma+mental+illness

This Is My Brave

Open call to submit to your own story. https://thisismybrave.org/
Provides for individuals sharing their mental illness stories.

Total Wellness

Employer mental health toolkit to break mental health stigma at work.
https://offers.totalwellnesshealth.com/mental-health

References

Angermeyer, M.C. and Matschinger, H. (2003), The stigma of mental illness: effects of labelling on public attitudes towards people with mental disorder. Acta Psychiatric Scandinavica, 1 08: 304-309.

Beals KP, Peplau LA, Gable SL. Stigma Management and Well-Being: The Role of Perceived Social Personality and Social Psychology Bulletin. 2009; 35(7):867-879.

Byrne, P. (2000). Stigma of mental illness and ways of diminishing it. Advances in Psychiatric Treatment. (1), 65-72.

Corrigan, P. W., Watson, A. C., Gracia, G., Slopen, N., Rasinski, K., & Hall, L. L. (2005). Newspaper Stories as Measures of Structural Stigma. Psychiatric Services, 56(5), 551–556.https://doi.org/10.1176/appi.ps.56.5.551

Crocker, J. (2002) Contingencies of Self-Worth: Implications for Self= Regulation and Psychological Vulnerability, Self and Identity, 1:2, 143-149.

Finlay, L. (2006) The body's disclosure in Phenomenological research, Qualitative Research in Psychology, 3:1, 19-30.

References

Lazowski L, Koller M, Stuart H, Milev R. Stigma and discrimination in people suffering with a mood disorder: a cross-sectional study. (2012). *Depress Re Trea* 2012;2012:724848. doi: 10.1155/2012/724848. Epub 2012 Apr 9. PMID: 22550571; PMCID: PMC3328894.

Mancini, M. A., & Rogers, R. (2007). Narratives of recovery rom serious psychiatric disabilities: A critical discourse critical discourse *Critical analysis. Approaches to Discourse Analysis across Disciplines*, 1(2), 35-50.

Markowitz FE. The effects of stigma on the psychological well-being and life satisfaction of persons with mental illness. *J Health Soc. Behav.* 1998 Dec;39(4):335-47.

Michalak, E. E., Yatham, L. N., Kolesar, S., & Lam, R.W. (2006). Bipolar disorder and quality of life: patient-centered perspective. *Quality of Life Research*, 15(1), 25-37.

Oral ET. Stigmatization in the long-term treatment of psychotic disorders. *NeuroEndocrinol Lett.* (2007).Feb;28 Suppl 1:35-45. *Quality of Life Research*, 2006 Feb15 (1):25-3.

References

Russell SJ, Browne JL. Staying well with bipolar disorder. *Aust N Z J Psychiatry.*2005 Mar;39 (3):187-93.

Watson, J., & Helou, M. (2006). Men'S Consumption Fears and Spoiled Identity: the Role of Cultural Models of Masculinity in the Construction of Men'S Ideals. *ACR Gender and Consumer Behavior.*

Wiglusz, M. S., Landowski, J., Cubała, W. J., & Agius, M. (2015). Overlapping phenomenon of bipolar disorder and epilepsy common pharmacological pathway. *PsychiatriaDanubina, 27 Suppl 1,* S177–S181 1, S177–S181.